Conversations with a Stranger. 2ⁿᵈ Edition

A Search for God

by Larry J Tate

Table of Contents

Introduction... *1*

The Encounter *3*

The Wager... *9*

The Mover *23*

The Beginning.. *35*

The Cause.. *51*

The Necessary *61*

The Perfect.. *75*

The Intelligent Designer...................................... *85*

The Greater... *97*

The Parting... *103*

The Revelation.. *109*

The Light.. *113*

The Mission *135*

Epilogue... *141*

Notes to the Text *143*

Introduction

This is a story of a man who grew up not believing in the existence of God. Without giving much thought to God, he just lived his life from day to day. If he were to consider the existence of God, he would need to be presented with absolute proof.

One day he had coffee with a stranger in a coffee shop. This encounter led him down a path of discovery about God's existence. During the course of several conversations with the stranger, he very well may have found some compelling proofs of God's existence. What he did not know was that he was about to stumble onto something he was not expecting to find, something that was far beyond anything he could imagine discovering.

"I have a story to tell. I have a question to ask. Please join me as I take you on my journey. There once was a day when I met this stranger..."

The Encounter

On any given day, you have the opportunity to make at least one new acquaintance. Nurture and cherish each acquaintance you make. Somewhere, somehow, someone is destined to have a profound effect on your life. Somewhere, somehow, you are destined to have a profound effect on the life of someone else.

The smell of coffee was in the air. Dishes were clattering. People were coming and going. My favorite coffee shop was of the local mom and pop variety. I didn't like the flash and pizzazz of the fancy chain stores. I was one of those who felt more comfortable with a down-home atmosphere. But times do change. Some time back, even my favorite shop had awakened and smelled the coffee. Now, they, too, were offering those high-end coffees with names I couldn't pronounce.

On this particular Monday morning, the coffee shop had its usual crowd. There were the loners like me, the early morning business meeting types, the health-conscious moms who wanted to treat their children to bagels rather than doughnuts, the internet junkies with their laptops, and then there were a few unfamiliar visitors.

I could always be found at the same coffee shop, at the same time, every morning. I had become a creature of habit. Every day I got up, got dressed, went to the coffee shop, sat at the same table, drank the same black coffee, ate the same whole wheat bagel, and then went off to work. To call me a man of habit would be an understatement. You could set a clock by my habits. I don't know if my obsession with doing the same thing day in and day out was due to my personality or due to my training. I had studied math, physics, and engineering in school. Somewhere along the way, I became one of those geeks with six different writing instruments in my shirt pocket. It was all I could do not to carry a slide rule in my pocket. Slide rules had been outdated for years, but I just could not resist the urge to use one.

I wasn't one to sample all the varieties of coffees offered at the shop. My only venture into fancy coffees was hazelnut coffee. Otherwise, my coffee was plain, and always black. My breakfast was a whole grain bagel with butter and honey. None of that fancy cream cheese for me. I felt more comfortable doing the same thing over and over again than doing something different.

My ritual included sitting at the same table for forty-five minutes, thinking about the long and tedious day ahead of me. My life reminded me of a movie I once saw in which the main character woke up on the same date, day after day after day. Every morning when he went outside, he saw the same people doing exactly the same thing as the day before.

All day long, I thought about numbers and the way things work. I was a fact-based person. I was more at home in a corner by myself than anywhere else. The last thing I wanted was to get involved with another person in idle chitchat. On the other hand, if someone wanted to talk about facts, science, and numbers, I was their guy. Otherwise, I could be found by myself, back in some corner.

Even though there were many familiar faces, I didn't know any of them. In fact, I don't think I can remember speaking to any of the other patrons during the entire time I had been visiting the shop. My only communication was an occasional hello to the counter help. The employees knew me and my unchanging pattern. When I walked through the door, they would place the same coffee and the same bagel on the counter. In like fashion, I nearly always gave them exact change, down to the penny. You can't get much more efficient than that.

After settling into my chair, I took a look around the shop. I saw a stranger walk in the door. He went straight to the counter and spoke to someone at the cash register. Then he started walking around the shop. I figured that they must have hired a new employee because he was walking up and down the aisles and around all of the tables, looking at each and every patron and smiling. *Perhaps he is a greeter*, I thought. I hadn't ever noticed a greeter before, but that concept seemed to be catching on. I doubted that he would last long though. He smiled at everyone, but never uttered a word. *Perhaps he's a bus boy*, I thought. *No, he can't be a bus boy. He isn't cleaning off a single table.*

It wasn't long until he made his way to my table. He smiled at me and said, "Good morning, friend. How are you this fine and wonderful day?"

Good grief, I thought. *He's one of those happy people.* He hadn't spoken to a single person before he got to my table. *Why did he choose to talk to me? Why can't I just be left alone?*

"Fine thank you," I answered.

"I'm mighty glad to hear that," he said. "This certainly is a great day to be alive. Wouldn't you agree?"

I mumbled something barely audible, hoping he would take my hint and move on.

After glancing up to the counter he said, "Well, friend, I believe my order is ready, so I've got to run along. It's been very nice talking to you."

Oh good, he's leaving, I thought. *I guess he's not a greeter after all.* The strange thing about him was that if he wasn't hired help, he certainly was being nosy.

After a bit, I finished my coffee and bagel. With one hand, I held my napkin just under the edge of the table. With the other hand, I carefully wiped the crumbs off the table and into the napkin. After neatly folding the napkin, I stuffed it into my empty coffee cup. On the way out the door, I put my cup, knife, and fork in the appropriate basket; threw the napkin in the trash; and placed my tray on top of the trash receptacle. Out the door I went to endure another day of mind-numbing number crunching.

The Wager

Everything I contemplate, and every decision I make, is a wager placed on my life. All too often and with too little thought, I take a frivolous risk on my health, my wealth, my family, my friends, and my life. I have determined to carefully consider each new action I take.

On Tuesday morning I found the coffee shop busier than usual. The shop was rarely ever full, but this day was different. I picked up a newspaper, went inside, and stood in a long line to order my coffee. As I turned around to leave the counter, I noticed that there wasn't a single table available. Toward the back, I spotted a lady who looked like she was nearly ready to get up and leave. Her bagel had been reduced to crumbs and her coffee cup was nearly empty. I drifted over near her table, not so close as to make her nervous, but close enough for me to grab the table before anyone else could. Shifting from foot to foot, I kept one eye on her and the other on nearby tables.

After a few minutes she got up and headed for the door. I was sitting in her chair before she could get two steps away.

Settling down, I began drinking my coffee and reading the paper. Before long, I felt a tap on my shoulder and heard a voice behind me saying, "Excuse me, friend, all of the tables are taken. Do you mind if I sit at your table while I wait for another table to open up?"

I turned around and saw the same stranger looking down at me with that same annoying smile on his face. I couldn't think of a good reason to turn him down, so I reluctantly said, "Sure. Have a seat."

After taking a sip of his coffee he began that idle chat I so disliked. It went on and on. First, he talked about the weather, then sports, then local news, then national news, and then world events. Trying to be polite I attempted to act interested, while in my thoughts I was wishing another table would open up so he would leave me alone. No such luck was with me that day. He discussed Afghanistan, Iraq, Iran, and Israel. He talked about the Gaza Strip and the West Bank. Then he started discussing the strife between the Israelis and the Palestinians.

In no time at all, he was talking about religion. I wasn't much of the religious type, so the more he talked, the more uncomfortable I got. "Sir," I interrupted, "I don't mean to offend you, but this religious business is something I really don't care to talk about. I haven't even made up my mind if there is a God or not. There are a lot of religious people out there talking about God, but to date none of them have actually shown me God. Now, if someone could definitively prove to me with pencil and paper that there is a God, I wouldn't mind talking about God. So far, I just haven't seen or heard anything to convince me that there really is a God."

"Really?" he replied. "If you don't mind my asking, how did you come by this way of thinking?"

I did mind him asking. But I had opened my mouth and he had responded. I didn't have much choice but to answer his question. "Well, my parents weren't very religious, so as a child, I rarely ever darkened a church door. As an adult, I just never gave religion much thought. My engineering background leads me to seek scientific proof for most everything I encounter. Facts and structure are the things that make me tick. If you can prove something to me, I'll believe it."

Unshaken, he took another sip of coffee and sat back. "Well, friend, I can see that you're the analytical type." He stared out into space for a few moments and then continued, "You know, I have heard about the works of some great religious thinkers. Some people call them Christian apologists or philosophers. The information I have is that some of them actually claim to *prove* that God exists. I have often wanted to explore their arguments. Perhaps you would be interested in delving into them with me. Who knows, maybe both of us could benefit from their knowledge and wisdom."

I knew I was in trouble. I had learned early in life that sales people have an answer for every excuse a potential customer can think of. It doesn't matter what reason you give for not wanting their product, they have a response to your objection. Consequently, I had determined that when sales people come by, I should never give them an opportunity to answer any of my objections. Generally, I had two or three responses, such as, "I'm not interested," or, "I don't want it," or, "Please leave me alone." Never did I give a reason for not wanting their product. I had become quite capable at cutting sales people off at the pass. It usually involved some rudeness on my part, but at least I could get rid of them rather quickly.

Yet in just ten minutes this stranger had tricked me into forgetting my tactics, and had lured me into giving a reason and excuse for why I didn't want to talk about God. It appeared that I had fallen into his trap and made myself vulnerable to his sales pitch about God's existence. *Okay*, I thought, *I might as well hear his pitch. Eventually, I'll be able to get out of this conversation and get on with my life.*

"Well, sir," I reluctantly replied, "I find it hard to believe that someone can prove that God exists, but why don't you go ahead and tell me about these so-called arguments and proofs you've heard of. I'm warning you, though; I want hard facts and provable arguments. I don't want any of that mystical mumbo jumbo."

He smiled, set his coffee on the table, and said, "Okay, friend, I'm cognizant of how critical and analytical you are. I'm not going to try pushing any of my own beliefs off on you. I'm just going to share with you the beliefs that others have spoken of. Then you can decide for yourself. How does that sound?"

I nodded without uttering a sound.

"Friend, do you ever place wagers?"

"Of course not," I said. Gambling was a subject I knew a little about. I had studied probability theory and the virtual guarantee that in the long run, gambling will always result in a net loss. "Sir, I don't have any desire to lose my money on gambling. I have better things to do with my money. Life itself is a gamble, and my investments are a gamble. That's enough for me."

"You're not afraid to speak your mind," said the stranger. "Can you tell me what the definition of a wager is?"

"That's simple," I said. "A wager is the act of placing a certain predetermined risk on the outcome of a certain event. Normally, a person puts down a certain amount of money in a game of chance with the hopes of winning a larger amount of money."

"Tell me, friend, have you placed any wagers today?"

"No, I have not," I bristled. "I don't squander my money. Have you forgotten that already?"

Acting as though he didn't hear me, he continued, "Just suppose, my friend, that you were to walk up to a gambling table and see that there are only two choices for you to bet on. You could place your bet on red or you could place your bet on black.

While you are looking at the table, the dealer tells you that if you bet on black, the best you could hope for was to break even but you're likely lose your entire bet. On the other hand, if you bet on red, the worst you could do would be to break even, but you're likely to win a large sum of money. Now, friend, what would you do?"

I chuckled at the stranger and said, "For one thing, no casino would ever offer such a bet. But there's no question about what I'd do. Black has no chance of winning, while red has no chance of losing. So, I would bet on red, as would anyone else who has a lick of sense."

Sounding as if he was changing the subject he said, "Tell me, friend, do you enjoy having your coffee here at this coffee shop?"

I answered, "Yes, I sure do. I come here almost every day. What's that got to do with placing a bet?"

Ignoring my inquiry, he continued, "Well, my friend, you came in a car, didn't you?"

Now, I was getting a bit irritated. He seemed to be drifting from subject to subject. "Of course, I came in a car. Otherwise, I'd still be walking."

"If you'll bear with me, my friend, surely you've heard of people being injured in automobile accidents. Wouldn't you say that there is more risk of personal injury while driving your car to this coffee shop as opposed to walking here?"

"You've got me there," I said. "Statistically, there isn't much risk in driving a car, but due to the speed of the vehicle, an automobile accident does have the potential for causing serious injury. On the other hand, walking exposes a person to less risk from injury. So…yes I suppose there's a little more risk in traveling by car than by traveling by foot."

"So, friend, you *did* place a wager today. You made a determination in your mind that you would incur a little more risk by driving a car so that you could have more time to do other things today. On the other hand, had you chosen to walk to the coffee shop, while being somewhat safer, you may not have the time to enjoy all of the other things you want to do."

"Okay, sir. You've made your point. I can see that I'm considering risks versus rewards in virtually everything I do. Now, sir, what's this got to do with placing a bet in a situation where I know in advance which bet loses and which bet wins, and what does all of this wager stuff have to do with the existence of God?"

I was getting flustered, but he was as calm as a cucumber. Continuing on, he said, "I'm going to tell you about a wager[1] you can make on the existence or non-existence of God. Once you see the wager, you may be convinced to believe in God without us having to go any further exploring proofs of his existence."

"Sir, are you telling me that by placing a bet, I will come to believe in God? That's the most ridiculous statement I've ever heard. For one thing, there aren't any wagers in which a person knows in advance which bet wins and which bet loses. For another, a wager can't even begin to prove the existence of God. Who in their right mind would make a bet on the existence of God?"

"You're going to be a challenge," he said. "But let's continue. Would you agree that there either is a God, or there isn't a God?"

"Yes, sir. That seems clear enough. There are only two choices regarding the existence of God. God exists, or He doesn't exist. Mathematically speaking, God has a fifty percent chance of existing."

"And, friend, would you agree that a person either believes in God or doesn't believe in God?"

"I'm not sure about that, sir. I am in another category all together. I told you earlier that I don't know whether I believe in God's existence or not."

"That's all right, friend. Let's see if that position deserves another category. Do you believe right now that God exists?"

With exasperation I exclaimed, "No, sir. As I said, I don't know if he exists!"

"So, friend, you're admitting that you don't fit in the *believing* category, aren't you?"

"No, sir, I don't fit in the believing category."

"Friend, it appears that your position of *not knowing* is in the arena of *not believing*."

"Why is that, sir?"

"When we say that a person either believes or does not believe, we are saying that there is a believing category and a negative of the believing category. While you may not be declaring that God absolutely does not exist, your *not knowing* is in the camp of not believing."

"Okay, sir, in that light I can see that a person either believes in God or doesn't believe in God. You are making me weary with these fine-pointed definitions."

"We have to make a solid case," said the stranger. "Now, try to imagine placing a wager on one's belief in God. What would be the risk you would be taking, and what would be the potential reward?"

I thought for a moment. The stranger had just taken me to a point I did not want to cross. I was being forced to provide an answer as though I was accepting the possibility of the existence of God. The stubborn side of me just did not want to give in to his argument. On the other hand, I was doing similar analogies every day at work by considering all sides of a particular problem. Feeling a bit relieved, I looked up at the stranger and said, "Well, I think we will have to make some certain assumptions first. Christians claim that after death believers go to heaven and unbelievers go to hell. Right now, I don't know if God exists, but for the sake of this argument I will use heaven as the reward and hell as the loss."

"That sounds reasonable enough," he said.

I pondered his question and said, "It appears to me that the wager placed is my belief or unbelief in God. And it appears that the reward or loss is what I encounter after my life has ended."

"So, can you describe for me the various outcomes of the wagers?"

"I believe so. There are only two choices for the wager. I can either believe in God or not believe in God. So, if I believe in God and He does exist, then I would go to heaven. On the other hand, if I don't believe in God, and He does not exist, I lose nothing; I break even. When I die, I will merely cease to exist."

"Okay, friend, but what if you do believe in God, and he does not exist?"

"That's easy. If I believe in God and he does not exist, I still break even. When I die, I will merely cease to exist."

"And finally, friend, what if you don't believe in God, but He actually does exist?"

"According to Christian teachings, I would go to hell after I died."

"So, friend, like the gaming table we spoke of a few minutes ago, this wager has but two choices. One bet, not believing in

God, has no chance of winning. The other bet, believing in God, has no chance of losing. If you were placing a wager on your life knowing that one of the wagers cannot possibly win, and the other wager cannot possibly lose, wouldn't you want to place your bet with believing in God?"

Staring into space, I took a few moments to analyze his logic. After considering his statements from every possible angle, I turned my attention back to the stranger. "I see your point," I said. "It seems to make sense on a certain level. And it certainly causes me to think a little differently about the existence of God. But still, this wager theory does not prove the existence of God. I would like to see the real proofs and evidence of the existence of God that you told me about."

"Certainly," said the stranger. "Your stubbornness is quite evident and overt. I would like to share with you some of those arguments and proofs. Would you like to start now?"

My time was beginning to run out. "Sir, I really need to go to work." Trying to be as polite as possible I said, "Perhaps if you and I meet again, we could continue this conversation." Then with politeness aside I continued, "But it's going to be an uphill battle to prove God's existence to me. You've got to be armed with a lot more than some silly wager scenario. As a matter of fact, why don't you bring God with you next time we meet?"

Without acknowledging my snide remarks, the stranger said, "Next time I see you, I'll be happy to talk about some proofs of God's existence."

I excused myself and left the coffee shop. I didn't know if I would ever see the stranger again. *Oh well,* I thought, *I really can't imagine that he could prove to me that God exists anyway.*

The Mover

I once thought it noble to be an immovable man. Stable as a rock I thought myself to be, until someone came along and moved me. It was then that I understood: an unmoving rock is not able to help my neighbor who is in need.

I once thought it noble to be an immovable man. Stable as a pool of calm water I thought myself to be, until someone came along and moved me. It was then that I understood: unmoving water so stagnant and foul is incapable of nourishing my neighbor in need.

I once thought it noble to be an immovable man. Stable as an oak tree I thought myself to be, until someone came along and moved me. It was then that I understood: an unmovable tree has no capacity to love my neighbor in need.

Somewhere, somehow, someone had the compassion and courage to move me. They filled my heart with encouragement, love, and support. Their mission was to help me. Now I understand that I am most noble when I help my neighbor who is in need.

On Wednesday, I went to the coffee shop at my usual time. I found the shop to be nearly as busy as the day before. My usual table was taken but I really didn't mind. I didn't want to make it easy for the stranger to find me again. I settled in at a table on the other side of the shop. I chose a chair facing the wall, thinking that he may not recognize me and move on to pester another patron. After patting myself on the back, I buttered my bagel, took a sip of coffee, and opened up my newspaper.

Before I got through the first paragraph of an interesting story, I heard a voice behind me saying, "Hello, friend. It's so good to see you again. Do you mind if I join you?"

What luck! He had found me in spite of my efforts to hide from him. While mustering up a fake smile, I said, "Hello, sir. Have a seat."

He didn't waste any time getting right into conversation. "Well, friend, do you have any thoughts regarding the wager theory we talked about yesterday?"

"It was rather interesting, in a strange sort of way. Sure, it caused me to think, but it doesn't prove that God exists by any means."

"You've made a fair assessment of the wager theory, my friend. I just wanted to begin our discussion with a thought-provoking theory developed by a great scientist who had a hand in the development of probability theory. Before we continue, I would like to interject one more thing for you to consider."

"What is that, sir?"

"People use elements of that scientist's probability theory every day in the arena of economics as well as gambling, but you're having trouble being convinced to trust his wager theory."

"You drive a hard bargain, sir. But I think I have good reasons for accepting his probability theory while rejecting his wager theory on God's existence."

"What is that, friend?"

"His probability theory actually works. It works both in theory and in practice. On the other hand, while his wager theory appears to be sound on paper, it cannot be proven in practice."

"It looks like I am going to have to work hard to convince you that God exists."

I felt a smug look creep across my face. Leaning back in my chair, I said, "Yes, sir, you've got your work cut out for you."

Without appearing to be intimidated in any way he said, "If you don't mind, we could continue today with the thoughts and ideas of another great person."

I figured I might as well go ahead and listen to him one more time. "Okay, sir, let's hear another one."

He smiled again and began with a probing line of thought. "Would you agree that at this very moment things are in motion?"

"Sir, I don't know what planet you're from, but on this planet, there are things in motion, and there are also things that are not in motion."

"Let's talk about those things not in motion right now. Would you agree that most everything either has moved or could be moved at some point in the future?"

"Yes, sir, it is reasonable that most anything has moved or could be moved." This stranger had a way of communicating thoughts and ideas without making me think I was being lectured to. It seemed as though he just asked questions and I ended up giving all the answers. His teaching methods were about as strange as he was.

"I suppose the same would apply to all matter that is out in the universe as well. Am I correct about that, my friend?"

"Yes, I suspect that everything out in the universe is moving, has moved, or can be moved. So, it appears to me that everything, no matter what or where, is moving or can be moved."

"Very good, friend. Can anything move its own self?"

I needed a little time to think. I didn't want this guy trapping me, but so far, he seemed to be straight with me. *Let's see,* I thought. *Obviously, a rock can't move itself. First something or someone must put the rock in motion. A tree can't move itself, but the wind can cause the leaves and limbs to move about; large earth-moving equipment could actually uproot the tree, putting it into motion. What else? A car won't move until some outside source puts a chain of events together, resulting in the car's movement. The planets move around the sun, but not due to their own power.*

"Sir, I don't believe any non-living object is capable of moving itself, and I suppose the same goes with plants. But the animal kingdom is a different matter. You asked me if anything can move itself. Well, I can move my own self, and most other animals are capable of moving themselves."

"Friend, you said that you are capable of moving yourself. Is your body a single unit, or is your body an organism made up of many individual biological parts?"

"Sir, I'm not sure if I am following you."

"That's all right, my friend. We are exploring this idea together. Let's see…okay, let's try it this way. A person might consider his car as a single unit, but is it not actually an assembly of many individual parts?"

"Yes, sir, there are thousands of parts that make up the total assembly of a car."

"Likewise, isn't your body just an assembly of many biological parts?"

"Well…I suppose it is."

"Can your fingers move on their own free will?"

"I don't believe they can, sir."

"Can your hands and arms operate as if they had a mind of their own?"

"No, they can't."

"And, before you begin walking, isn't there something other than your legs that causes your legs to begin moving?"

"I hope you're coming to a point, Sir."

"Yes, friend, I am. Wouldn't you agree that your brain must send certain signals to your various body parts before those parts are capable of moving?"

"Okay, sir. I give up. It appears that you're right."

"And then there is the brain itself. Can your brain send those signals without some outside influence?"

"Sir, I believe that the brain is the command center of all that goes on in the body."

"Can the brain operate without an ample supply of blood and oxygen being sent to it by other parts of your body?"

He had me there. "Sir, I stand corrected. It appears that nothing, not even an animal, is capable of moving itself. And it appears that even my brain is dependent upon some outside influence. It sounds to me that some outside force is needed before anything is able to move."

"I believe we are getting somewhere, my friend," said the stranger. "Is there such a thing as perpetual motion?"

If this stranger wanted to push off his philosophies on me; he was going to have his hands full. I knew enough about how things work to ensure that he would not be able to pull the wool over *my* eyes. The concept of perpetual motion has intrigued mankind for ages. There is just one little problem that gets in the way. Friction cannot be eliminated. No matter how slight, friction will eventually stop anything that is in motion.

"No there isn't," I replied. "Perpetual motion is impossible. Eventually, everything put into motion will cease its motion without the continuing influence of some outside source."

"Okay, friend, it appears that any object in motion had to have some other mover to put that object into motion. And, likewise, there had to be some other mover farther in the past to put that mover into motion. This sequence of moving and being moved goes farther and farther in the past. Now, friend, I think we are about to be confronted by a problem."

"What is that, sir?"

"I can imagine the first object ever moved, but I'm having trouble figuring out what moved the first object."

"Well, sir, the first object moved was moved by the first mover."

"Friend, that sounds logical, but didn't the first mover also need a mover?"

"Oh, now I see the problem."

"Yes, friend, it looks like we've come up against a brick wall. We know that every object that moves needs a mover. We also know that every mover also needs a mover. Somewhere back at the beginning of time, there had to be a first object in motion. We know that to be a fact. But that first object in motion could not have begun moving without a mover moving it. We can imagine the first object in movement, but what about the mover of the first object in motion? What moved the first object? What was the first mover? How could the first mover move the first object if the first mover had to be moved itself?"

Now my head was spinning. It was simple enough to think that everything moving was caused to move by something else immediately in its past. But the complication arose as we looked farther and farther in the past. I retraced our conversation in my head. The more I thought about it, the more unsure I became. How can there be a first mover, if something was required to move *it*? If that were so, it would not be the first mover.

"Sir, I'm a bit confused. I guess I just haven't had enough time to think about it. I agree with you that we've encountered a problem with the first mover, but there must be an answer. Tell me, what do you think caused the first object to move?"

"Friend, in the universe, everything that moves must have something other than itself to move it. Likewise, the first object to have ever moved, no matter how far back in the past, also had to have a mover that put *it* into motion. We know that perpetual motion does not exist. Nevertheless, there still had to be a first mover. So, whatever it was that put the first object in motion could not have been a part of the universe. The very first mover had to be something that did not have something farther in its past to cause it to move. What do you suppose that could be?"

Talk about mixed emotions! I had absolutely no desire to consider the existence of God, but somewhere in the dark corners of my scientific mind, I was enjoying this stranger's tactics. Nevertheless, I had no idea what the answer to his question could possibly be. In exasperation I said, "Sir, the only conclusion left is that the first mover must be an *unmoved* mover. I don't know how that can be, but it must be so."

"I believe you are right, friend. The one and only conclusion is that there must be an unmoved mover."

"Okay, sir, now what? Where does that leave us?"

"We have determined that the first mover is an unmoved mover.[2] The unmoved mover cannot be a part of the universe. This *unmoved mover is none other than God Himself!*"

There it was! He told me that he thought he could prove that God exists. We walked through a series of logical conclusions and ended up with the ultimate conclusion that God must exist. This stranger was making me think of things I had never considered before. His logic seemed to be sound, but was it good enough to prove to me that there actually is a God? I still couldn't *see* God. With all of his so-called proof, I still couldn't bring myself to believe that there really is a God. *There must be an objection to this conclusion,* I thought.

Weakly, I argued back, "Sir, I think you're making an assumption that the universe had a specific beginning. I've heard it said that the universe is infinitely old. What do you say about that?"

"You might have an argument there," he said. "Why don't we explore that idea together? After considering some facts we already know about the universe, perhaps we can come to a reasonable conclusion regarding its beginning."

I seriously doubted that we could solve the mysteries surrounding the beginning of the universe while sitting at a coffee shop table. "Sir," I replied, "this has been a most curious conversation and I would love to explore the beginnings of the universe. But, I need to leave for work before I get fired. That would cause my personal universe to fall apart. Perhaps we could talk more on this subject if we happen to meet on another day."

"Friend, I am honored that you would like to continue discussing things with me. I'll certainly look forward to it."

With that, I excused myself and hurried off to work.

The Beginning

For after all, what is man in nature? A nothing in relation to infinity, all in relation to nothing, a central point between nothing and all, and infinitely far from understanding either. The ends of things and their beginnings are impregnably concealed from him in an impenetrable secret. He is equally incapable of seeing the nothingness out of which he was drawn and the infinite in which he is engulfed.

Blaise Pascal

On Thursday morning I was able to reclaim my regular table. Apparently, the conference or whatever it was that came to town was over. I didn't bother trying to hide from the stranger this time. I was beginning to learn that he would find me no matter where I seated myself. About the time I got comfortable in my chair, I heard the familiar greeting, "Hello, friend." I didn't even have to turn my head to see who it was.

His hands were full. In addition to a coffee cup filled to the brim, he was carrying two saucers, one with a bagel and the other with a doughnut. Inevitably, he spilled part of his coffee on the table. By instinct, I immediately reacted by jumping out of my seat before any of the hot coffee could land in my lap. In short order, we were able to clean up the mess and sit back down at the table. With a silly grin on his face he said, "I sure made a mess, didn't I?"

"Well, sir, it happens to all of us."

"It sure does. How are you doing on this beautiful day?"

"I'm fine, sir."

He began buttering his bagel, drinking his coffee, and chatting incessantly.

I just let him continue on, occasionally giving him an "oh," or a "yes," or a "hmm." It seemed as though this guy just enjoyed listening to himself talk.

Eventually he had to stop and catch his breath. After a moment he asked, "Friend, what were we talking about yesterday?"

Grateful for a change of topic I said, "Well, you suggested that there had to be a first mover, and you determined that the first mover must be an unmoved mover. You went so far as to say that the unmoved mover could only be God. Then we began discussing the beginning of the universe."

"Oh yes," he said. "You must be keeping notes. But don't forget, friend, we came up with those conclusions together."

"The last conclusion was yours, sir."

"Perhaps, my friend, but it does bear consideration, does it not?"

"I will keep my mind open, sir."

"That's good enough for me, friend. Well now, what do you think about the beginning of the universe?"[3]

"Sir, I haven't burned up many of my brain cells dwelling on the beginning of time, but I've heard a couple of theories. One is that the beginning goes back to infinity. Another is that the universe had a definite beginning. As far as my opinion goes, I tend to lean toward the theory that the universe is infinitely old."

"Okay," he said. "That is as good a starting point as any. Let's just explore some known facts and see if we can agree on a logical conclusion."

"Sir, do you really think that two regular guys like us can figure out the beginning of time right here in this coffee shop while sitting at this table?"

Chuckling, he replied, "You don't appreciate the brain power you have, my friend. But who knows what we can accomplish until we try?"

"Okay," I sighed. "Let's get started."

"Perhaps we should first agree on the meaning of the term infinity," he said.

"That's an easy one for me," I said. "Infinity is an unlimited and unending extent of time or quantity."

"Unlimited and unending..." he pondered. "Okay, so if the universe is infinitely old, then the beginning must extend backwards toward the past, down an unlimited and unending extent of time prior to today. Is that right?"

"It sounds like we are off to a good start," I said.

"Okay. To help us understand an infinite amount of time in the past, let's talk about something simpler first. Let's talk about numbers in general."

"You're the teacher, sir."

"Friend, I would like to think that we are doing this together. I pose a question, and you answer. You pose a problem, and together we will work out that problem."

"If you say so, sir."

"Now back to numbers…if it is possible to count forwards for a certain number of units, wouldn't you agree that we must also be able to count backwards to the point of beginning?"

"Sure enough," I replied. With my background, math was an easy subject.

"And likewise, if it is possible to count backwards for a certain number of units, wouldn't you also be able to count forwards back to the point of beginning?"

"I don't see any problem with that assumption either," I said.

"Friend, pick a number."

"Pick any number?"

"Yes, any number is fine."

"Okay, my number is 823."

"823? How did you pick that number?"

"I don't know, sir. It just came in my mind. Is there a problem with that number?"

"Any number is fine. I was just curious about where that number came from. It's a bit strange, but we can work with it."

I thought, *Why is he calling me and my thoughts strange? He makes himself at home at my table, talking about all kinds of weird stuff, and he thinks I'm strange?*

Continuing, he said, "Okay, we'll start with the number 823. Now, if we were to count forwards for another hundred numbers, we would get to 923. Is that right?"

"Yes, sir."

"Now that we are at the number 923, is there any problem with counting backwards until we get back to our original number of 823?"

"No problem, sir. If it is possible to count forwards to some certain number, it is certainly possible to count backwards to the point of beginning, whatever number the beginning happens to be."

"All right, friend, if instead of counting forwards from 823 to 923, what if we were to try counting backwards from 823 to 723?"

"Sir, there wouldn't be a problem doing that either. We can count back to the number 723 and then count forwards back to the original number of 823."

"Great, friend. You are helping me immensely. Now, what if we were to try counting backwards from the number 823 all of the way to zero? Could that be done also?"

"No problem, sir."

He looked toward the ceiling as if he was counting the ceiling tiles. Then he said, "Let's consider the first moment of the universe. Is it conceivable to imagine the first moment of the universe?"

"Well, that would be a long way back there, but I suppose a person could imagine the first moment."

"But, friend, you said that the universe may be infinitely old, and that infinity is an unlimited and unending extent of time. If the beginning is infinitely in the past, then the very first moment must always be farther and farther back in the past, beyond any moment previously identified as the first moment. So how could the very first moment ever be identified?"

"Hmm…sir, you have a point there. Now that you put it in that kind of light, I doubt that the very first moment could ever be identified."

He tapped his fingers on the table, considering his next words. "Okay, so you say that the first moment in an infinite past cannot be identified because by the time you could get to what could be conceivably identified as the first moment, you would just find that the actual first moment would still be farther in the past. Am I right?"

"I believe so, sir."

"Consequently, the definition of an infinite past simply does not allow for a first moment."

"That looks to be the case, sir."

"Help me out, friend. Wouldn't the beginning of time be considered as moment number zero?"

"Well, sir, technically the first moment would be moment number one, not moment number zero. But, I understand your point. Just before moment number one should be moment zero."

"Okay then, Mr. Know-It-All. Let's call the first moment, moment number one."

For just a brief moment, I wondered if his last remark was some sort of an insult. But his big, crooked smile easily disarmed my negative notions regarding his intentions. I relaxed a bit and said, "Okay, sir."

"Friend, if the first moment is always farther and farther in the past, then it appears that there may be a problem in assigning the number one to the first moment."

"We may be on to something, sir."

"We've already determined that it is possible to count from any given number back to the number zero. But if the first moment is elusively farther and farther back in the past, I don't see how it would be possible to count back from this present moment to the very first moment in an infinite past. As a matter of fact, it is quite impossible to count back to the first moment if the beginning is infinitely far in the past."

"I don't have any problem with that assumption," I said.

"Okay, we've determined that we can't identify the first moment. Consequently, we can't attach the number one to the first moment. So...since we can't identify the first moment, perhaps we could identify the second moment. Do you think it would be possible to identify the moment that occurs after the first moment?"

I thought for a little bit and said, "When considering a series of moments, it seems logical to me that the second moment should be identifiable, but if the first moment can't be identified, then I don't believe that the second moment would be identifiable either."

"So," said the stranger, "it sounds to me like you are saying that if the first moment can never be identified due to it being infinitely far in the past, then by default, the second moment would also be infinitely far in the past. Okay then, let's go farther up the ladder. What about the third moment?"

"Well, sir, if there is no identifiable second moment, it doesn't look to me that there could be an identifiable third moment."

"Let me get this straight," mused the stranger. "If you can't count back from today to the first moment and if you can't count back to the second or third moments, it would appear to me that you also could not count back to the fourth, fifth, or sixth moments. Is that right?"

"We *are* talking about infinity, sir."

Continuing on he said, "If you can't count back to the moment after the first moment, then you also can't count back to the next moment after that or the next moment after that or the tenth moment or the thousandth moment or even the millionth moment. This hard thinking is about to singe the hair on my head."

"Yes, sir, mine too."

"Now, friend, if I had ten beans in a row, one of those beans would be the tenth, one would be the ninth, one would be the eighth, and so on, right down to the first bean. We can count back to the first bean because the beans had a beginning. But, in the case of an infinite past, there aren't any first, second, third, fourth, fifth, or sixth moments. Likewise, there can't be any tenth, hundredth, thousandth, millionth, or billionth moments. Am I right?"

"I can't fault your logic, sir."

Without saying a word, the stranger got out of his seat and started walking around the room, looking at the other coffee shop patrons. He went to the window and gazed outside for several minutes. I had given up on understanding this stranger, so I just sat there drinking my coffee and eating my bagel. After a long while, he came back and sat down. Without saying a word, he gave himself a vicious pinch on the arm. "*Oweee*," he yelled out.

Embarrassed, I looked around to see if he was disturbing other patrons around us. Fortunately, everyone seemed to ignore him. "What are you doing, sir?" I whispered.

Ignoring my question, he asked, "Friend, would you pinch yourself too?"

I was getting a little exasperated with him. I was accustomed to sitting in a corner and being somewhat invisible. This guy's antics were compounding the risk that unwanted attention would be drawn to me. "No, I will not pinch myself until you tell me what is going on."

"I'm right here!" he exclaimed. "I'm here…and this coffee shop is full of other people who are here. I am right here…in the now and the present, along with a room full of people. I just wanted to find out if you're here too."

Indignantly I retorted, "I don't have to pinch myself in order to know that I'm here. What is your point, sir?"

"Well, friend, it looks like we just proved there's no such thing as an infinite past."

"*What?*" I exclaimed in a startled voice. "What does pinching ourselves have to do with proving that there is no infinite past?"

With a look of triumph, the stranger smiled at me and said, "If time past goes back to infinity, then we and our universe could not and would not exist. The present time can exist only if it is a step in the future from an immediate step in the past. But, if time past goes back to infinity then step number two has not yet been reached. If step number two has not yet been reached, then steps three, four, five, and six have not been reached. If step six has not been reached, then the tenth, hundredth, thousandth, millionth, and billionth steps have not yet been reached. So whatever step we are in, here in the present, could have never been reached. As a matter of fact, if the beginning of the universe goes back to infinity, then the beginning has not yet occurred. If time past goes back to infinity, then there actually is no such thing as time. Consequently, this current moment right here in this coffee shop can never be reached. If time past goes to infinity, then you and I would not be sitting here right now, pinching ourselves and acting silly."

Still feeling the burning in my face from being embarrassed by his recent outburst, I replied, "Respectfully, sir, only one of us is acting silly...and it isn't me."

Still smiling he said, "Maybe I'm getting a little too excited about what we just discovered."

He then leaned across the table and pinched me on the arm before I had time to pull back. I flinched and sat up straight, looking at him with evil eyes. My arm was stinging, and a red spot was beginning to form. Still smiling he continued, "If time past goes to infinity, we would not be sitting here right now. But, the fact is...we *are* sitting here right now; we *are* pinching ourselves. The only logical conclusion left is that time and our universe definitely did have a beginning."

I was stunned and speechless. I didn't know if I was more shocked at his conclusions or the fact that he had taken the liberty to reach across the table and pinch me. I had never thought of time like that, but it certainly did made sense. This stranger seemed to be able to solve one of the mysteries of the universe right there in the coffee shop, while sitting at the table.

After a little bit I said, "You may be right. It appears that the universe did begin at a specific time."

"It's not just me, my friend. We did it together."

With foggy eyes, I looked around the room and out into the parking lot. After recomposing myself, I glanced back to the stranger. He was busily munching on his bagel. Here we were, struggling with the mysteries of the universe, and this stranger was just gobbling up bagels and slurping coffee as if he didn't have a care in the world.

After an uncomfortable silence he said, "What a relief to know there is no such thing as an infinitely old universe. If it was, we wouldn't be able to enjoy our coffee today. And this bagel is just too good to miss out on. Isn't it fun solving age-old mysteries of the universe?" With his mouth half full of bagel, he cheerfully said, "You know, friend, life is just about the greatest thing there is." Then with a chuckle he uttered the old cliché, "It certainly beats the alternative. What do you think?"

Sometimes, this guy seemed to be so far out in left field that he should be institutionalized. Then at other times, he seemed to be able to look straight into the heart of a very complicated matter. I sat back in my chair and just stared at him with a puzzled look on my face. I just didn't know what to make of the guy sitting across the table from me.

After downing his coffee, he said, "Friend, we went off on a tangent discussing the beginning of time. I believe we can get to the bottom of several other proofs that God exists. I've got plenty of time if you do. Are you ready to get back on track and discuss another proof?"

I couldn't make up my mind if I enjoyed having discussions with him, or if I hated them. In one way, I was aggravated at the way he had elbowed his way into my life, but at the same time it was rather intriguing to follow his arguments to their conclusion. I looked at my watch and was surprised at how fast time was passing by. "Oh my, look at the time. I've got to run, sir. Maybe I should take a rain check on that offer."

Without the slightest hesitation, he said, "No problem, my friend. The next time we meet, we can talk about the first cause."

I didn't have a clue what he meant by the first cause, but I was confident that he would have some profound explanation for it. I was already late for work so I said good-bye and excused myself. As I was walking out the door, I turned around and saw him go up to the counter and order another cup of coffee, along with the biggest bagel they had. Shaking my head, I headed off to work.

The Cause

You and I were created. Having been created, we have become creators. Every action we take and every word we speak influences the behavior and actions of another. Someone somewhere will act according to the example they have seen in us. In some small way, we are contributing to the way that others will walk out their own lives. Likewise, they will influence others still. The way in which our actions mold other people will be passed down to countless others for many years to come. As creators, we have a great responsibility. We should approach every action we take and every word we speak with great thought and humility. We all leave behind a legacy. We all leave behind a creation. What are we creating today? There is an eternal record kept on each and every person. Each of us is writing our own autobiography. God created us in His image. Are we building up others and encouraging them to stay in His image, or are we tearing down others and discouraging them from emulating His image? Every action we take and every word we speak is molding and creating the character of another. Our actions and words are powerful tools. Are you using your tools of creation to do good?

As habit would dictate, I entered the shop at my regular time, bought my same black coffee, and proceeded to my favorite table. Not long afterwards, the stranger came through the door, bought his coffee, and found his way to where I was sitting.

He stretched his arms up high and took a deep breath. As he exhaled, he let out a pleasant sigh. Then he cheerfully said, "Top of the morning to you, my friend."

"Hello, sir," I said. "Have a seat." This fellow was just too happy and optimistic for me. I wondered to myself, *Doesn't he ever have the same old boring and routine days like everyone else? He's too young to be retired, but he never seems in a hurry to go to work. What's up with this guy?* In spite of my questions, I didn't ask any for fear that he would want to reciprocate by asking personal questions about me. Not that I had anything to hide, I just didn't like opening up to other people.

"I am so glad to see you again," he said with that same permanent smile.

His smile reminded me of music show personalities. All through the show they have a great big smile plastered on their faces. I often imagined them eating and sleeping and even shaving with that huge abnormal smile. I usually got more enjoyment out of those imaginations than I did from their actual shows.

I was brought back to reality when he said, "If you like, we can continue our conversation, and talk about another proof that God exists."

"Sure," I said. "Day before yesterday we discussed that every object in motion needed a mover. That was interesting and thought provoking. Some people might actually find it to be convincing, but I still have my doubts. I'm not easily swayed by every seemingly logical statement that comes my way. What else do you have that I can sink my teeth into?"

"Well, I don't know if I can promise to give you the absolute answer you want, but I do have more proofs to share with you." He stopped talking, took a sip of coffee and began looking around at others in the coffee shop, saying good morning to them. They must have been as self-centered as I was, because they pretty much just ignored him and continued to eat their bagels and drink their coffee as if no one else was in the coffee shop. Or maybe they thought he was the strangest person on the planet and simply ignored him. The brush off by the other patrons didn't seem to affect him at all. He turned back to me and asked, "Did your coffee cup make itself?"

What a strange question. He said he was going to talk about God, but instead he asked if my coffee cup was capable of making itself. "No, it didn't make itself. Anyone with a lick of sense knows that."

"If the coffee cup didn't make itself, then who or what made the coffee cup?"

"Well, sir, a machine made the coffee cup."

"A machine?" he pondered. "Now this machine you are speaking of…did *it* make itself?"

"Now, you're playing games with me," I said. "No, sir, the machine didn't make itself either."

"Okay, friend, you're saying that the coffee cup didn't make itself, and the machine didn't make itself either. Now then, machines are made up of many parts, right? Perhaps the parts made themselves. What do you think, friend? Do you suppose that the various parts of the machine created themselves?"

"I don't know where you are going with this, sir. No, the parts of the machine could not, did not, and never will make themselves. Do you have a point to your madness?"

"As a matter of fact, I do. The coffee cup didn't make itself. The machine that made the coffee cup didn't make itself. The parts in the machine didn't make themselves either. It just makes you want to scratch your head in wonderment, doesn't it?"

"Yeah, yeah, I'm just scratching my head until it bleeds. Continue on, sir. Please make a point before I lose my mind."

"Oh yes…I believe there is a point to my line of questioning. Everything that exists was created or caused by something else. That something else was an object or entity that already existed.

Friend, herein is our dilemma. As we go farther and farther back in time, we should eventually reach the first thing that was created or caused. Is that right?"

"I don't see the dilemma, sir. What is so confusing about the first thing caused or created?"

"Well, friend, perhaps you can help me with my confusion. Everything in existence needs something else to cause or create it. So, when we get to the very first thing in existence, we should be able to determine that something was the cause of that very first thing. But if every cause is also in need of a cause, then what caused the first cause?"

"Now, you've got me thoroughly confused," I said. "You must stay up all night dreaming up these riddles. How do you ever get any sleep?"

With a belly-rocking laugh he answered, "I'm not losing any sleep at night, but thanks for the concern. It certainly can be confusing. It's almost like asking which came first, the chicken or the egg. If the chicken came first, then we wonder how the chicken came into existence without first hatching from an egg. If the egg came first, then we are in a quandary about where the egg came from, because an egg can only come from a chicken."

My mind began drifting. I really didn't have any concern about how much sleep he was getting. As a matter of fact, it was rare for me to feel such emotions for anyone, much less this stranger who had befriended me. I knew he was just being polite, but all too often politeness tends to be little more than a façade. On most any day of the week, someone will ask me how I'm doing. Before I have a chance to open my mouth and answer, they are moving on and talking to someone else. To me, politeness is highly overrated.

Back to the task at hand, I continued our conversation. "All right, I see our dilemma," I said. "How can we dig our way out of this one? What caused the first cause?"

"Well, let's just dig a little deeper. Nothing can begin to exist on its own power. It must have a prior cause before it can begin to exist. We've already determined that the universe and everything in it had a beginning. The first thing in the universe had to have had a cause. That is a fact. So, there must be something that is not a part of the universe that caused the universe and everything in it to come into existence."

I had to protest his last statement. "Sir, there can't be something that is not a part of the universe. The universe is the accumulation of everything that is. Outside of the universe there is nothing. Anyone should know that out of nothing comes nothing. So, how can there be something that is not a part of the universe? Quite obviously, something can't be a part of nothing." I leaned back with the confidence that I had stumped the stranger.

"You bring up a valid objection," he said. "Let's try it from another angle. Everything that exists was caused by something else. Anything and everything that ever came into existence was not capable of making its own self but had to be caused by something that already existed. Going back in time, we find a chain of caused objects preceded by the causes that created them. Eventually, we must find our way to the very first object that was caused. This first object *must* also have a cause. We now know that the universe had a definite beginning. And we know that everything that is must be caused by something that already exists. The only conclusion left is that there must be a first cause that is *uncaused*."

Repeating himself he said, "Everything that exists was caused by something. That something was caused by something else. So, everything that ever existed had to have been caused by something else that was previously caused. If there was no uncaused cause, then the first thing that came into existence had to come from nothing."

"Sir, I think you are baiting me. I guess I'll go ahead and bite in spite of my better judgment. Something can't come from nothing. That is impossible."

"Well, if something can't come from nothing, then we are left with the one and only conclusion that the very first cause had to be uncaused. The uncaused cause had to exist outside of the universe of material things. But the uncaused cause also must be something. It can't be nothing."

"Are we getting somewhere, sir?"

"Friend, I do believe we have arrived. The uncaused cause is not a part of our universe of material things, and the uncaused cause is not a part of nothing. Friend, I think we have stumbled onto the solution to our problem. Day before yesterday, we discovered that the first mover had to be the unmoved mover, called God. Today we have determined that the first cause must be *the uncaused cause, called God.*[4] This uncaused cause is not a part of the universe. This uncaused cause is outside of time. The uncaused cause has no beginning, and it has no end."

I found myself regretting the day I crossed paths with this stranger. Up until then, I felt fairly confident about my beliefs. He was causing me to doubt myself and question most everything I had previously settled in my mind. "You know," I said, "I can't think of an objection to your so-called proof at this very moment, but there must be one. Your conclusion seems to hold water, but I just can't see how it absolutely proves the existence of God. It sure would be convenient if I could just see God. Then I would know for sure that he exists."

"You are stubborn, indeed," he said. "I'm sure that this proof is not an absolute proof, but it sure sounds convincing to me. Since we got to the bottom of the First Cause, perhaps we could explore another proof."

"Not today," I said. "My cup is empty, and it's time to go to work. It appears that you're beginning to become a regular patron here at the coffee shop. Perhaps we can continue the next time we meet."

"You're the boss," he said with a big smile of his face. "I'll look forward to our next chat. If you don't mind, I'm going to just sit here a little longer and have another cup of coffee."

"No problem," I said. "I'll see you later."

The Necessary

Only one thing is necessary: to possess God.

Henri Frederic Amiel[5]

On Monday morning, the stranger was already seated at my table when I walked in. In a sense, he was no longer a stranger. We had been having regular encounters and conversations. He certainly didn't treat me like a stranger, not even on the first day we met. But I wasn't anxious to take our relationship to the point of being friends. Being more comfortable on a formal basis, I hadn't even asked his name, and so far, he hadn't asked mine. As I approached the table he said, "Good morning, my friend."

"Hello, sir."

"Being alive is about the best thing there is. Don't you agree?"

"Well, it's better than the alternative," I replied. "It sounds like things are going good for you, sir."

"*I'm just great!*" he resounded. "If life was any better than this, I wouldn't be able to stand it. How was work Friday?"

"Every day is just like the day before," I moaned.

"Well, I think you're in for a great future. I don't know why I think so, but I just feel it. Can you feel it?"

"Not really, sir."

"You'll come around, I'm sure. Start imagining yourself doing what you want to do and feeling the way you want to feel. Start imagining that the answers to life's questions are right in front of you, waiting to be seen and understood. Pretty soon you will come to believe what you are imagining. After you imagine something and believe it, you will eventually begin doing the things necessary to achieve it. Soon, you will find yourself possessing it."

I wasn't sure if he was feeding me some sort of mumbo jumbo or what. It wasn't the first time I had heard that sort of philosophy, but I never had given much consideration to it. I decided to file it away in my mind and reconsider it at a later date.

While I was mulling over his last statement he asked, "Are you ready to see if we can discover another exciting proof of God's existence?"

"I didn't realize that the first two proofs were exciting. But yeah, let's hear it."

"Well, I for one can't wait to get started." He didn't waste any time getting right into the subject matter. "I'm sure you'd agree that you, yourself, exist."

"Well, that seems easy enough to answer, sir. I saw myself in the mirror this morning while nicking myself with a dull razor blade. So yes, I believe that I definitely do exist."

"Can you exist in a vacuum chamber?"

"No, sir, I need air to breathe. Besides that, my eyes would probably pop out of their sockets if I was in a vacuum."

"Can you exist without food?"

"No, I can't. My body needs the nourishment provided by food in order for me to survive."

"So, it appears that the survival of your body is contingent upon other things and other factors."

"You have no argument from me," I said.

Without hesitating, he continued, "It looks like you are telling me that your body can exist only if something else also exists right now, at this very moment."

"Sir, I believe that to be true. Our bodies require the influence and impact of other things in order to survive."

He leaned back in his chair and twiddled his thumbs. After a few moments he asked, "Friend, what exactly, are you?"

He had a strange way of communicating his ideas. "What am I?" I asked. "I'm a human, of course. The last I checked, I wasn't in the jelly fish family."

His perpetual smile grew even bigger. "Well, whether you are a human or a jelly fish, wouldn't you say that you definitely are a material being?"

"No one has accused me of being a ghost, sir."

Ignoring my sarcasm, he asked, "And wouldn't you say that you are a limited being, as opposed to an infinite being?"

"Sir, we decided previously that the term infinite implies something of an unlimited and unending nature. So yes, I am a limited being."

"Finally, friend, are you a changing being?"

"Of course, I'm changing. I have a picture of myself when I was twenty-one years old. I certainly don't look the same today as I did then. And then there are those aches and pains. I didn't have them when I was twenty-one either. And then there is the problem with my hair. When I was twenty-one, I had lots of hair on my head. Today, that hair is on my back and in my ears. So, yes, I am a changing being. I'm not too happy about it, but that's the way it is."

"Friend, you are about the funniest person I know. Anyhow, you're admitting that you are dependent upon other factors, and that you are a limited and changing being. What else do you suppose is limited and changing?"

"Well, everything in the animal kingdom is limited and changing."

"Is that all?"

This guy didn't make things easy for me. Far be it from him to volunteer much information. He acted like he wanted me to come up with all of the answers. Who was teaching whom? "Well, sir, I reckon that everything in the plant kingdom is also limited and changing."

"Is that all? Is there anything else?"

While waiting for me to think about his question and respond, he was busy drinking his coffee, eating his bagel, and glancing about the room. He was beginning to get on my nerves. There were times when he reminded me of when I used to play chess with my father. Being a youngster and not having much enthusiasm for becoming intimate with the intricate strategies of chess, I would have to sit for minutes on end laboriously thinking about each and every move. Not being one to sit idly by, my father would keep busy reading a book, changing channels on the radio, or talking to others in the room. The more he did that, the more frustrated I got. Eventually, and with much hesitation, I would make my move. Out of the corner of his eye, he would see me retract my hand from the game board. With speed and flair of authority, he would then move his piece. Then the whole frustrating process would start all over again for me.

My eyes must have glazed over while I was reminiscing about my past. I had completely forgotten what he had asked. "I'm sorry, sir. My mind must have drifted off. What did you ask me?"

"Not a problem, friend. You said that both plants and animals are limited and changing. I asked you if anything else is limited and changing."

"Oh yes, now I remember. I'm not sure what else is also limited and changing. But I suspect I will know shortly."

"I am referring to inanimate objects. Take rocks for example. Do you suppose that rocks are limited too?"

"That's simple enough to answer. Yes, rocks are limited too. They're not infinite by any means."

"Wouldn't you agree that most everything on earth is limited?"

"Sure. Why not? Everything on earth is limited."

"What about the planets and stars? Are they limited?"

"Well, the only other choice is unlimited or infinite. So, my vote is for all planets and stars being limited too."

"Bear with me, my friend. I certainly do appreciate your patience."

Patience is necessary indeed, I thought. I needed a lot of patience to listen to this fellow every day.

"Since the universe is the total accumulation of all planets, stars, and all other matter, wouldn't you say that the universe and all that is within it is limited?"

"You drive a hard bargain, sir. Sure, why not? The entire universe is limited."

"Perhaps you would also agree with me that the universe and all that is within it is also changing."

I was beginning to understand the negative feeling that most people have with attorneys. Like this stranger, an attorney continuously builds his case one statement at a time until his victim is backed into a corner with no way out.

"Sir, I've got to protest. I don't know that I can agree on the changing part. A rock doesn't change. It's inanimate. How can a rock change?"

"Have you ever hit a rock with a hammer?"

"Yes."

"Did it break?"

"Yes."

"So, it changed, did it not?"

"If you put it that way, I guess so."

"What about the sun and the stars? The very act of giving light and heat requires change doesn't it?"

"I suppose so."

"Now, there is other matter in the universe. There are planets, asteroids, comets, and no telling what else drifting about in the universe. Do they not change whenever they are impacted by other matter floating about in the universe?"

A bit irritated, I protested, "Sir, you won't quit until you win. Yes, it seems that the entire universe and all that's within it is limited and changing in some form or another. What else do you want from me…my first born?"

Undeterred, he continued, "Now, my friend, let's recap a little bit. The existence of every human, every animal, and every plant is contingent upon something else for its very being. Without something outside of themselves, they would not have come into existence. Without something outside of themselves, they would not continue to be in existence. Without something outside of themselves, they could not change."

"I believe that is what we agreed on."

"And all other matter, while not living and breathing, is dependent upon something outside of itself to cause it to change in the way that it changes. All matter and the entire universe, living or not living, is dependent or contingent upon something else."

"It sounds like we are going in circles again, sir. You remind me of a guy who has one foot nailed to the floor and all he can do is walk in circles. But yes, you seem to have a point."

"You are quite comical, my friend," chuckled the stranger. "Your existence is contingent upon something else. The existence of that something else is contingent upon something else yet. This contingency goes on and on and on. It goes farther and farther back in the past to the very beginning. We already discussed that there is no such thing as perpetual motion. Likewise, there can't be an entire universe of contingent beings that are all dependent upon other contingent beings for their existence and change. Everything that exists needs to be given being, but at some point in the past, there must be something that was not contingent on something else."

"I feel like I've been here before, sir. I think you're getting ready to make a point."

"Yes, I believe we are working our way up to a point. There must be something that is not and cannot be contingent on something else. From our description and definition of the universe, this something cannot be the universe itself, and it cannot be any part of the universe. This something that is not dependent or contingent upon something else can only exist in itself. It must be something from outside the universe of matter and limited beings. But what is outside of the universe?"

"We have previously determined that there is nothing outside of the universe."

"Can nothing have an influence on something?"

"No, sir. We've made a determination on that also. Nothing is nothing. Only something can have the capacity to influence something else."

"We have arrived at another dilemma, my friend. All matter is contingent upon something else for its existence and/or change. But beyond the beginning of the universe, there was absolutely nothing. Before there was something, there was only nothing. If nothing has no capacity to create or change, then the universe could not have begun to exist. Yet, my friend, the universe did begin to exist. So, there must be a *necessary being* that is not contingent upon anything else for its own existence. There must be something that exists, something that does not exist on the condition that something else gives it existence. There must be something that exists only in and of itself. The only thing required for this thing's existence is this thing itself. There must be a necessary being that is not a part of the universe. There must be a necessary being to cause the being of all contingent beings. All of creation cannot owe its being to its own self, but to something other than itself. All of creation had a beginning. If all of creation had a beginning, then there was a time in which it was not. All of creation and all parts of creation could not have created themselves. All of creation was the result and influence of some other necessary being that was not made or created. This *Necessary Being is God.*" [6]

"Kudos to you, sir," I said while slowly clapping my hands in mock applause. "You've done it again."

"No, my friend, *we* have done it again, you and me together." Continuing as if I had not just insulted him, he said, "So far, we have explored several proofs of God's existence. He is the Unmoved Mover, He is the Uncaused Cause, and now He is the Necessary Being. Our two simple minds have proven that God exists. How do you feel about our discovery?"

"As I stated before, these proofs are thought provoking indeed. As convincing as they are, they still don't absolutely, and without a doubt, prove that God exists. At the risk of sounding defiant, I wonder if you have any other proofs."

"You ask and I provide," replied the stranger. "Yes, my friend, I do have more. Let me think…oh yes, I've got another good one. It goes like this—"

Quickly, I interrupted him, "Wait a second, sir. Time is getting away from me again. Will you be here tomorrow?"

"If you're going to be here, I'll make a point to be here also, friend. I look forward to sharing another proof developed by a great thinker."

Getting up I said, "Sounds like a date. I'll see you tomorrow."

The Perfect

God is the perfect poet, who in his person acts his own creations.

Robert Browning[7]

On Tuesday, I was tired and cranky. Lightning, thunder, and pounding rain outside my window kept me awake nearly all night. It didn't help matters that when running to my car I stepped in a deep puddle of water and soaked my feet and pants.

When I arrived at the coffee shop parking lot, I reached under my seat for my umbrella. After stretching and straining, I finally found it. It was one of those compact umbrellas that fit in the palm of your hand when not in use. It looked pretty practical when I saw it on the store shelf. But on that particular day, I was about to regret my choice of umbrellas. I slammed my car door and began trudging across the parking lot toward the coffee shop. Suddenly, a gust of wind turned my umbrella inside out. By the time I got to the protection of the shop's sidewalk awning, I was soaked from head to toe. I carefully reset my umbrella to its original shape, folded it up, and left it near the door.

The stranger was standing by the window watching others make a mad dash to the protection of the canopy over the sidewalk. "You look like a drowned rat," he said without making any effort to hide his laughter.

"I feel like one too. What a sloppy day."

He joined me at the counter while I waited on my coffee, but he didn't order anything for himself. "No coffee for you today?" I asked.

"Can't pass up my morning coffee," he said. "But mine is already at our table."

I jerked my head toward him with a mixture of surprise and disgust on my face. He was talking about *our* table as if we were the best of friends. I didn't say a word. Instead, I just meekly followed him over to *our* table.

Sure enough, when we got to the table, I spotted his coffee and a half-eaten cinnamon roll. Leaning against his chair was the most massive umbrella I had ever laid eyes on.

"You won't get very wet with that umbrella," I said.

"It certainly is a good one," he replied. "I don't enjoy getting wet like you do, so I bought the biggest and best umbrella I could find." Again, he started laughing while pointing to my wet and dripping clothing.

I pretended that he never even made that remark. Instead, I just stared at my coffee.

After some silence, I glanced up and noticed that he was looking out the window at the still-pouring rain. "Not as nice this morning as yesterday," he said.

"No, it certainly isn't."

"You know, there are bad days, not so bad days, good days, and not so good days. Then, you hear people talk about the absolute worst days or the most perfect sunny days."

"Yeah and today is one of those not so good days," I said.

"And then there are flimsy umbrellas, there are lousy little folding umbrellas like yours, and there are fantastic umbrellas like mine." This time he didn't bust out laughing, but he sure did have a big grin on his face.

"It sounds like you just insulted me, sir."

"Oh. I'm sorry," said the stranger. "I didn't mean to insult you. I was just talking about how some days are better than others and how some things are better than others."

"Next thing I know, you're going to start talking about how much uglier I am than you," I retorted.

"Now, I wouldn't do that," he said. "But now that you mention it, some people are better looking than others. Have you ever heard someone say that they saw the most beautiful woman in the world? Or have you ever heard someone refer to the ugliest person on the face of the earth?"

"Are you going somewhere with this insanity?" I asked.

"As a matter of fact, I am. If you are ready, I would like for us to explore another proof of God's existence based on what we've just been talking about."

How can he do that? I thought. Just a casual conversation about the weather can turn into another proof of God's existence.

"So, discussing my little flimsy umbrella and a rainy day is sufficient enough to prove that God exists. I've got to hear this one. Please go ahead, sir."

"Since you insist, I believe I will," replied the stranger. "We've already noted that some days are better than others, and some umbrellas protect you from the rain better than others. We also agreed that some people have a better physical appearance than others. You know, virtually everything we see and do has a certain degree of quality based on the best or worst of its kind. One bed is softer than another; one light bulb is brighter than another; one shade of paint is whiter than another. All of those comparisons are based on the best of that particular quality. All of those comparisons are relating to degrees of perfection. Beauty is a certain degree of perfect beauty. On the other end of the scale, homeliness is also a degree of perfect beauty…just farther down the scale." He paused, took a sip of coffee, and made an ugly face. "You know, my coffee isn't as hot as yours because it's been sitting on this table for quite a while. I think I need to pour it out and get a refill. If you will excuse me, I'll be right back."

Before he took two steps, he paused and looked back at me with a smile. "You know, it just hit me…I was just referring to the various degrees of hot coffee. Your coffee is hotter than mine. Yours is closer to the ultimate for hot coffee, and mine is farther down the scale for the perfect temperature of hot coffee." Without another word, he spun on his feet, heading for the coffee counter. I could hear him chuckling as he went. This guy was just too happy for me.

When he returned, I said, "You seem like a nice guy, but sometimes you talk about the strangest things."

Without any hesitation he said, "Speaking of being a nice guy, I guess you're comparing me to some people who are not so nice, some who are very nice, and some who are downright mean. It sounds like you have just compared me to others, in degrees of perfect niceness."

"Well, sir, I suppose so."

Continuing, he said, "And then there are degrees of goodness, degrees of knowledge, degrees of color, and even degrees of prosperity, wouldn't you agree?"

"All right," I said. "Everyone and everything has qualities that are of various degrees of perfection for some particular quality."

"How discerning," he answered. Are you sure you don't already know where we're going with this discussion?"

"Believe me," I replied. "I don't have a clue where we're going."

"All of the things we've discussed are thought of as more or less of a certain quality that is considered to be the ultimate of that particular quality. That ultimate quality is the perfect quality."

"I'm anxious to see how you can tie this into the existence of God. Quite frankly, I am amazed at how you've been able to do it so far."

"Not just me, my friend. We have done it together."

"Sir, I don't think we've done it together. You already knew all of the information we discussed."

"Not exactly, my friend. I was aware of the basic premise for each proof, but you and I worked our way through each of the proofs together. Quite frankly, my friend, I am mighty glad to be able to glean some scientific reasoning from your point of view."

I wasn't too sure if I had just received a compliment or not. "You are kind, sir. But I'm still not sure where we are going with this."

"We're just about there, friend. Let's recap a little bit. There's the perfect day that we compare every day to, there's the perfect umbrella by which all umbrellas are judged, there's a perfect beauty, a perfect brightness, a perfect whiteness, a perfect color, a perfect heat, a perfect courtesy, and a perfect goodness. We could sit here all day and never exhaust all of the qualities that are gauged against the ultimate of their respective qualities."

"That sounds perfectly logical to me. Oh…pardon the pun, sir." Here I was, the most boring person in the whole wide world, actually having a little fun myself.

Then I realized that I was thinking in degrees of perfection. I was referring to myself as the most boring person, as opposed to an entertaining person. And I was thinking of having a little fun, which is less than a lot of fun.

"Now, we have to think a little deeper. We've been discussing degrees of perfection. Somewhere there must be a most perfect color blue and somewhere there must be the brightest white. Someone must possess the greatest amount of goodness and there has to be someone whose face is the most beautiful face of all faces. But can those perfections be found? We know that for every perfect color found, we will eventually discover an even more perfect color. For every beautiful face, we will someday find an even more beautiful face. How can we solve our problem and determine the most perfect of all those qualities?"

"I'm lost, sir. Do you have an answer? Oh, what am I saying? You always have an answer."

"Great people have studied this problem. They have, in fact, uncovered the answer to the most perfect quality. Are you ready?"

"I'm on the edge of my seat, sir. What is it?"

"The universe and all that is within it is made up of material objects. There can never be an ultimate best in material objects because there will always be a better quality found at a later date. There also cannot be a most perfect trait in the universe because there will always be an even more perfect trait show up at some point in the future.

"There must be a most perfect of qualities by which all qualities are judged. This most perfect of all qualities is *the most perfect*. However, *the most perfect* cannot be a part of this universe.

"*The most perfect* that possesses the most perfect of all aspects and all traits must be outside of all that is. *The most perfect* cannot be the universe or a part of the universe. The most perfect being cannot be of material substance. *The most perfect* must exist in and of itself. In order for *the most perfect* to exist in and of itself, *the most perfect* must be *the most perfect being*. This most perfect being must be perfect in its own self and judged by its own self. *This most perfect being; this perfect one—is God.*"[8]

I was flabbergasted. This stranger could really make a case. And every time, he did it without any written reference material. How did he do it?

"That certainly is thought provoking, isn't it, friend? So far, we have proven that God is the Unmoved Mover, the Uncaused Cause, the Necessary One, and now the Perfect One. That's not bad for a couple of average Joes, is it?"

"Sir, you are too modest."

"Friend, I couldn't have done it without you."

I raised my coffee cup to my lips and discovered that it was empty. Time was running out, so I told him that I needed to leave. He wished me well and told me that he was going to stay awhile and have some more coffee. I excused myself and walked out the door.

The Intelligent Designer

The earth, the sun, the moon and
the stars, all objects of beauty,
complexity and vastness—are but
reflections of an intelligent
designer.

On Wednesday, just as I was about to go through the coffee shop door, I heard a voice coming from the courtyard. It was the stranger saying, "I'm out here, friend. It's such a pretty day, why don't we sit outside?"

That wasn't my pattern, but conversing with this stranger for the past several days wasn't my pattern either. "Sure," I said. "I'll be back as soon as I get my coffee."

With coffee and bagel in hand, I went back outside and sat down. It was a little bit windy and my napkin started drifting across the table. Quickly, I reached out and grabbed the napkin just before it fell into the stranger's lap. As I was about to retract my hand, he noticed a scar on my finger. "I hope you don't think

I'm being nosy, but I see that you have quite a scar on your finger. Do you mind telling me what happened to your finger?"

I thought, *Do I think he's nosy?* I almost snickered. This guy had decided to be my friend without any encouragement on my part. Now, he was looking out for my health. Is he nosy? You bet he is.

Looking down to see what he was referring to, I saw the scar. I had nearly forgotten about the injury. "Oh, that. A couple of months ago, while repairing my gas grill, my hand slipped against a sharp component of the grill. It nearly cut my finger to the bone."

"Did you go to the doctor?"

"No, I'm not into that medical stuff. Doctors and dentists scare me to death. I would rather take a beating than to go to a doctor."

"But you said you were cut to the bone. To me, that sounds serious enough to require medical attention. At the very least, you needed a tetanus shot."

"Probably so, but I did my own doctoring. I looked in my bathroom cabinets and found antiseptics and butterfly bandages. Then I closed up the wound and gave it time to heal. I don't think it looks any different than it would have if a doctor had taken care of it. There were other nosy people who were also chiding me for not seeing a doctor, too." Uh-oh. I just had a slip of the tongue. Telling a little white lie, I continued, "Oh, I'm sorry, sir. I didn't mean to imply that *you* were being nosy.

With a broad smile on his face he said, "No offense taken."

"Well, sir, like you, they were acting concerned and suggesting that I could end up with a dangerous infection or a horrible-looking scar. But here I am, healthy and whole."

"Thank goodness for that," he said. "It sure is nice that your body is capable of healing itself of so many potentially dangerous infections and diseases. Your body is an amazing self-healing machine, isn't it?"

Before I could open my mouth to answer he continued, "You closed up the wound with a bandage and then watched as your body knitted the wound back together. Have you ever considered just how proactive your body is in destroying potentially life-threatening attacks? Do you realize that this activity goes on continuously: minute by minute and day by day?"

"No, I haven't given it much thought."

"Exactly," he said. "There are literally hundreds and thousands of potential disease and infection attacks on your body every day. If you had to think about a response to each and every one of those attacks, you wouldn't have time for doing anything else. Your body is designed to keep itself healthy with little or no conscious thought on your part. Just think of the contaminants in the air you breathe. And then, nearly every time you put something in your mouth, you are also swallowing innumerable bacteria that would just love to ravage your body. Thankfully, the various defense mechanisms in your body just automatically identify, attack, and destroy all of those harmful intruders."

"Interesting," I replied. "I wish my computer was that efficient. I'm always dealing with a computer virus."

"Yes, friend, as smart as computers are, they don't stand a chance against the complexities and abilities of the human mind and the human body."

"Perhaps so, sir."

"Now, I'm not saying that you shouldn't see a doctor. A doctor, along with the medicine he gives you, assists your body in healing itself, sometimes at a much faster rate. The medical world has done wonders in eliminating many serious diseases."

"I suppose you're right, sir. There certainly does seem to be a lot more disease in third-world countries than there is here at home."

"Yes, we have a lot to be thankful for. Speaking of disease and sickness, have you ever wondered why they say there is no cure for the common cold?"

"Come to think about it, that certainly is strange. They can just about eliminate polio from the face of the planet, but they can't do much about a simple thing like the common cold."

"Well, friend, I don't know if it's true or not, but I've heard that the common cold may never be eliminated."

"That's interesting. I've got a feeling that you're getting ready to tell me why. I'm eaten up with suspense, sir. Let's hear it."

"From what I hear, the common cold is the body's way of cleaning house."

"That makes no sense to me, sir."

"Think about it for a second. You vacuum a carpet, because over time the carpet accumulates dirt, dust, pet hair, and everything else you can imagine. Your vacuum cleaner removes all the dirt for you. However, if you don't empty the bag, the vacuum cleaner will eventually lose suction and quit cleaning the carpet. Likewise, I've heard some people claim that your body *also* cleans house. The contaminants you breathe and swallow need to exit the body in some way or another. If they can't be expelled properly and quickly, your body will give you what is known as the common cold. For two or three days you cough, sneeze, and blow your nose. Could it be that your body has just cleaned out its vacuum cleaner bag? I don't know, but it sounds logical to me."

"Sounds far fetched to me, but who knows, maybe it's true."

"And then, there's the fever. There are those who say that your body develops a fever to burn out and destroy harmful organisms in your body. I'm not a doctor, but that sounds reasonable also."

"Are we having all of this discussion because I've got a scar on my finger?" I asked.

"Yep, you're right," he said. "Whether the common cold theory or the fever theory is true or not, it's still true that your body is an amazing healing machine. Wouldn't you agree with that?"

Wearily, I agreed.

Without any sign of slowing down, he continued, "Your body is one complex organism, doing many things at once with little or no conscious effort on your part, right?"

Before I had a chance to respond, he continued, "Your body is one single biological unit, but on closer examination a person would have to admit that the human body is able to function only because many organs and other body parts are working in cooperation and in unison with each other. While the heart's only function is to pump blood, it depends on signals from the brain to determine the rate of its pumping action. Even though the heart has no direct contact with the kidneys, it must supply blood to the kidneys so that they might do their own function for the health of the body. If the heart failed to supply blood to the kidneys, the kidneys would fail to do their part. If the kidneys failed to do their part, the heart would ultimately fail. So, the kidneys are dependent on the heart, but the heart is dependent on the kidneys. It gets confusing doesn't it?"

As usual, he had my mind going in circles. It seemed as though every subject he talked about gradually went to the impossible premise that everything is dependent on something else.

"Think about your vision," he said. "You don't even think about the effort involved in order to cause your eyes to function properly so that you can enjoy looking at nature. Your brain tells your eyes to focus on your cup of coffee. Then in an instant, when you decide to look up at a tree, your brain instructs your eyes to change shape and focus on the tree. Like your body, your eyes are made up of many intricate mechanisms that all work together in an intelligent manner so that you might be able to see the tree." Without missing a beat, he continued, "Your body is an amazing biological machine. Your body is made up of many interconnected, dependent organs. The organs are made up of specialized tissues and cells. The cells are made up of molecules, and the molecules are made up of atoms. Each and every step we take toward the most basic parts of our bodies, we find materials that are working together in an efficient and intelligent manner for the good of the greater."

"I didn't know I was meeting you this morning for a biology lesson," I said.

"Well, with me you never know, do you? It appears that the wonders of your body can prove that there is a God."

Here we go again, I thought.

He continued, "The way your body works and the way every part of your body works together can only be accomplished by an intelligent order. Like the relationship between the heart and the kidneys, if any interdependent part of an organ fails to do its part, other parts, and the body as a whole, will suffer. The only way such interdependence can exist is by way of intelligent design. Design doesn't just happen by chance. Design is the product of a designer.

"The universe and everything in it operates the way it does because of its design. Since everything in the universe is dependent upon something else in some way or another, there must be intelligent design.

"This intelligent design cannot be a part of the universe because the entire universe operates as a result of intelligent design. There must be something that is not a part of the universe that intelligently designs all that is within the universe. There must be something that is designed in and of itself and requires no outside influence for its own intelligent design."

He stopped and sat back in his chair for what seemed like an eternity. The ensuing silence allowed my mind to consider his latest statements. I could not deny the fact that the components of the universe seem to have the uncanny ability of working together as if they were designed to do so. Although I didn't have any strong feelings regarding the existence of God, his argument certainly did cause me to wonder about the possibility of some sort of intelligent design. I didn't have anything more to add, so I just waited for his next words.

Presently, he said, "There must be a non-designed intelligent designer. This non-designed designer must be designed in and of itself. It cannot be designed by any other outside influence. There must be an Intelligent Designer of this universe and all that is in it. *The Intelligent Designer is God.*"[9]

He had done it again. It seemed that every time he came to one of his deep and mysterious conclusions, he would break out in a great big smile as if he was patting himself on the back for how smart he was.

"You make a good argument," I said. "I don't know if I'm more intrigued with the subject matter of your arguments or your techniques for building a case."

"I take that as a compliment," he said. "You are very kind."

I hadn't made up my own mind if I was being kind to him or not. How many days was I going to have to listen to this stranger? I really liked the coffee shop and I didn't want to try out a new one, but it seemed that as long as I continued to frequent this particular shop, I was going to have to deal with him.

Time was beginning to slip by and I needed to leave for work. I told him that his intelligent designer argument was somewhat interesting, but not interesting enough to sway my opinion one way or another.

Unaffected by my candor, he smiled at me and continued drinking his coffee. I didn't know if I could ever hurt his feelings. My remarks just seemed to go right past him as if I hadn't said a word. As a matter of fact, he seemed to get friendlier than ever before.

The Greater

Love is God's essence; power but his
attribute: therefore is his love greater
than his power.

Richard Garnett[10]

Like clockwork, I showed up at the coffee shop on Thursday at my usual time. Like clockwork, the stranger was there too. What more could he find to talk about? Not to worry, I was sure he had plenty more material to try out on me.

I was in a big rush on this particular day. An early appointment was on my mind. My boss had instructed me to meet with him before I did anything else. He didn't tell me what the meeting was about; he just said to be there. I didn't do well with changes in my pattern, but deal with it, I must.

I must have been squirming in my seat because he said, "You look like you're in a hurry this morning."

"Yes, sir, I am. I've got an early meeting scheduled today. I'm sorry, but I can't stay long. I guess I won't be able to hear another of your proofs that God exists. I've got to drink my coffee quickly and run. I'm sorry, sir."

"I understand," he said. "It's important to take care of business." Hesitating, he said, "I was really looking forward to another discussion on the proofs of God."

"It doesn't look like it'll work out for today...unless you've got a really short one."

"Actually, I think I do. Maybe five minutes' worth."

There I went again. I had given a reason for not wanting to listen to him, and he had an answer to my objection. "Okay. It'll take that long to drink this hot coffee anyway. Go ahead, sir."

"I'll get right to the point, my friend. I know you haven't made up your mind if there is a God or not. However, for argument's sake let's consider the concept of God. In your mind, could you imagine anything, or any being that would be greater than God?"[11]

"No, I cannot. If there actually is a God, there couldn't be a greater being. If there were, then he wouldn't be God."

"So, my friend, it looks like you're admitting that the concept of God can and does exist in your mind. Is that correct?"

"Yes, sir, the concept of God exists in my mind."

"And even though you personally haven't made up your mind about it, could he actually exist in reality?"

"We are exploring all options anyway. Yes, God could exist both in my mind and in reality. Now, sir, that doesn't mean to imply that I think he really does exist."

"I understand, my friend. Okay, now suppose that he exists in your mind, but *not* in reality. Then, my friend, a greater than God *could* be thought."

"Why is that, sir?"

"Because a God existing in reality is greater than a God existing only in your mind. Am I correct in that assumption?"

This guy was really good at throwing out statements and questions that required a lot of thought before answering. I considered his proposal. We had agreed that when considering the concept of God, one must determine that a greater than God could not be thought. He threw a monkey wrench in my thinking when he suggested that we assume that God exists in our minds but not in reality. In such a case, there would be a violation against our concept of God, because it would then be possible to think of a God existing in reality, even though he actually does not exist in reality.

"Sir, I believe there is a problem with your last statement. We've already determined that a greater than God cannot be thought. An assumption that he does not actually exist in reality would go against our concept of God."

"Friend, I believe you are on to something. I guess it would be impossible for God to exist only in our minds. We have already determined that it would be impossible to think of anything greater than God. If God existed only in our minds, we would be able to imagine that God also exists in reality. Imagining a God who exists in reality would be imagining a God who is greater than a God who just exists in our minds. Friend, do you know what we have just done?"

"No, sir, I don't. What have we just done?"

"We have just proven that God must exist in both our minds *and* in reality."

"How do you do this, sir?"

"It's not me, my friend. We did this together. We used our own thoughts, wisdom, and deductive powers to prove that God exists. That grey matter between our ears has been hard at work."

"Let me get this straight. If I can imagine the concept of a God in which nothing is greater, then by default, he must also exist in reality. Is that what you're saying?"

"It's not just me, friend. You and I are both saying that."

"Don't put me in the God-believing camp just yet, sir. For such a short session, you have given me a lot to chew on. I am not one to make fast decisions. I like to look at everything from every possible angle. Sir, there are a lot of angles to the things we have been discussing. If and when we actually prove without a doubt that God exists, I will be the first to embrace that concept."

I looked at my watch and realized that the meeting with my boss was quickly approaching. I slid my chair back and stood up. "Sir, I'm sorry for leaving so quickly, but I've got to get to my meeting. Although you may *believe* that God exists both in your mind and in reality, I know for a fact that my boss exists both in my mind and in reality. If I don't get to that meeting on time, my job may no longer be a reality."

Chuckling, he said, "All right, my friend. Business is business. I hope it is a good and profitable meeting. I'll see you tomorrow."

The Parting

We only part to meet again.

John Gay[12]

I rushed to work and hurriedly parked my car. I knocked at my boss' office door and said, "Good morning, sir." Did you wish to see me?" My face reddened. Why did I ask that? I knew he wanted to see me, and he knew that I knew that he wanted to see me. The last thing he told me the day before was that he wanted to see me. "I'm sorry, sir. I knew you wanted to see me. I'm just a little flustered this morning."

"Sit down," he said while motioning toward a chair. "We've got a lot to talk about."

As I nervously found my seat, I wondered, *What could this be? Surely, I'm not in trouble. I'm the most trustworthy employee he's got. All of my reports and assignments have been complete and on time. What else could it be?* The reddening in my face began to be replaced by an ashen white, caused by the intense fear that gripped me. *I'm being fired,* I thought. *What will I do? Where will I go? This is the only job I've ever had.*

Interrupting my racing thoughts, he said, "Bill, you may have heard that we're starting a new office on the East Coast."

With a stammering voice I answered, "Yes, sir, it's been rumored about for some time now."

"Well, Bill, you are my most trusted employee. I want you to go to the new site, get it set up, and running."

I wasn't in trouble. What a relief. Color began to come back into my face. My shaking hands began to stop quivering. I relaxed a little and repositioned myself in my seat.

"I don't know how long it will take, Bill, but I would guess a couple of months—four at the most. What do you think?"

Four months? I thought. *Good grief. I don't like living out of a suitcase.*

Lying, I said, "Sir, I am honored that you would consider me. I will do my best. The good of the company comes first."

"Great, Bill. I knew you would be a team player. As a matter of fact, I've already arranged for your flight. You're leaving at nine o'clock in the morning."

What a price to be a team player, I thought. "Sir, that's not much notice."

"I know, Bill. I really am sorry, but this thing came together quicker than I anticipated. But, I know you will be able to pull it off."

"Okay. I'll be on the plane."

"Thanks, Bill. I'm depending on you to make us shine. Good luck."

I didn't share his enthusiasm as I left the office, but I didn't let him know about it. I went home and began packing my bags. Just before going to bed, I noticed the notes I had been making after each meeting with the stranger. At the last moment, I threw the notes in my suitcase. Four months is a long time. I figured that I might as well go over those notes and see if they can make any more sense to me.

On Friday morning, I got up a little earlier than usual. I figured I might as well have one last cup of coffee at my favorite coffee shop. I knew that by coming early, I would miss the stranger, but we weren't exactly buddies anyway. He would just have to get over it. Besides that, we hadn't even exchanged names.

After arriving at the coffee shop, I ordered my coffee and sat down by the door. I wanted to take in all of the familiar sites of home before leaving. I had no more than taken my first sip of coffee than who walked in the door, but the stranger.

"Hello, friend. You're here early today."

I was surprised to see him at the coffee shop this early in the morning. "Yes, I am," I said.

Since he was there, I decided that I might as well explain what was going on and why I wouldn't be back at the coffee shop for a while. "Sir, I'm afraid our conversations must come to an end."

"Friend, have I offended you? If I have, I would like to make things right."

"Oh no, you haven't offended me. I honestly can't say that I have been enthused about your proofs that God exists, but you may be delighted to know that I have taken notes on every one of them. Actually, sir, my boss surprised me yesterday with the news that I must leave town on business for an extended period of time."

"Oh, was that the important meeting you had to get to?"

"Yes, sir, it was. I really don't know when I will be back. Sir, I can't say that you've convinced me to believe that God exists, but I plan to examine my notes a little closer while I am gone. Whenever I do make it back home, perhaps we could continue our conversations. Do you live nearby?"

"No, friend, I don't actually live here. I'm just passing through."

"Oh, I'm sorry," I replied. "It looks like we may never meet again."

"Don't worry about it, my friend. I've enjoyed the conversations we've had together. I just hope you have enjoyed my company as much as I've enjoyed yours."

I didn't understand how he could consider me to be a good conversationalist. I mainly just listened to him and answered his questions. You meet all kinds of people during your life. This guy was one of those that causes you to scratch your head.

I couldn't be as enthusiastic as he was, but I tried to be cordial. I wished him well and got up to leave the coffee shop.

He embarrassed me when he also got up and gave me a massive bear hug. "Take care," he said. "You've been a joy to talk to." I nervously glanced about the room to see what the other patrons thought about me getting a lingering hug from the stranger. I was relieved to see that they didn't give us any glaring looks of surprise.

The Revelation

I believe in order to understand

St. Anselm[13]

I looked over my notes during the first few days at the new job site. I had a bad habit of being too detail oriented. Not only had I entered all of my notes on my laptop computer, but I had even titled my notes as if I was writing a book. Sitting there on my nightstand was a neatly stapled stack of notes entitled, *Conversations with a Stranger.* Sometimes I had to shake my head at myself when wondering why I did the things I did.

His assumptions and conclusions regarding the existence of God did seem to make a lot of sense. And they could be quite convincing to someone who was not as analytical as I was. But he was not dealing with the average Joe. He was dealing with me. Still not convinced, I put the notes back in my suitcase.

Days came and went. Each time I left the motel room, I would notice a Bible on the lamp stand by the door. One evening, finding myself rather bored, I glanced over at the Bible.

It caused me to think about my conversations with the stranger. He had said that his proofs were not actually his own proofs. Instead, they were the products of great men from the past. Not once had he mentioned a proof from the Bible. That struck me as odd. Normally, Christian fanatics point to the Bible to back up and prove virtually everything they are promoting. Was that stranger one of those Christian fanatics? If so, why didn't he refer to the Bible? If not, why did he care about proving God's existence? I was beginning to wonder about the stranger. He didn't seem to fit either category.

I decided that since I was stuck in a motel room for no telling how long, I might as well read the Bible. It would be interesting to see what it had to say about God and His existence.

I tackled my Bible reading just like everything else I did. I read it from cover to cover; frontward and backward. I even went so far as to make my own flash cards. Starting with page number one, I began reading and taking notes. Days turned into weeks. Weeks turned into months. I ended up being gone from home a little more than four months. During that time, I had amassed many notes taken from that motel Bible. Although the Bible was interesting indeed, I was not able to find any absolute proof of God's existence in the Bible.

One night before going to bed, I labored over my notes one more time. I just couldn't find anything to point to, and definitively state that I had finally proven that God exists. I went to bed that night thinking about my quest. My mind drifted to all of the Bible characters who claimed to know God. It seemed as though they had a certain peace and stability about them. It seemed as though they had a purpose that defined their lives.

Before going to sleep, I murmured to myself, *I don't know if God exists but if he does, I sure would like to know him the way those people did.* Finally, a fitful sleep overtook me. I tossed and turned for hours. Suddenly, I woke up and bolted to a sitting position. Had I heard a knock at the door? I raced to the window and looked outside. No, it wasn't anyone at the door. I went back and sat down on the edge of the bed. My heart was pounding and my mind was racing. I had been awakened by my own thoughts. I can't say how it happened, but a common theme from my Bible notes was playing itself out in my mind over and over again. I tried going back to bed, but I couldn't clear my mind.

Finally, I got out of bed, turned on my light, and began typing furiously on my laptop computer. By morning I was exhausted, but satisfied. Out of the hundreds of pages in the Bible, the truth of God's existence along with His plan for me was staring me in the face. How could I have missed it all those years?

. . .

A week later, I wrapped up business on the out-of-town project and arranged to go back home.

The Light

To one who has faith, no explanation is necessary.
To one without faith, no explanation is possible.
Thomas Aquinas

For God so loved the world, that he gave his only
begotten son, that whosoever believeth in him
should not perish, but have everlasting life.

John 3:16, KJV

On the first morning back home, I returned to my favorite coffee shop. The person behind the counter did a double take and said, "Where have you been? I thought you had left us."

"I just had to leave town for an extended business trip. I'm back now…for good, I hope."

"I'm trying to remember; you're a black coffee and bagel man, right?"

"Yes, you're right."

"Here you are. Have one on the house and welcome back."

"Thanks," I said as I headed off for my favorite table. Then I stopped in mid stride. I no longer desired to be in a dark corner of the coffee shop by myself. Spinning on my feet, I headed toward a table near a window.

This time, instead of just drinking my coffee and staring off into space, I found myself busily reading over my Bible notes. This was a refreshing change to my routine. In the past, I usually nursed my coffee while dreading the long day of work ahead of me. This time, I felt energized. I even caught myself locking eyes with other people and smiling at them.

While engrossed in my reading I heard a strangely familiar voice ordering coffee at the counter. *Surely not,* I thought. The stranger told me he was just passing through. What would he be doing here four months later?

I turned around, saw that he had already discovered me, and was making his way to my table. From thirty feet away he hollered out, "Good morning, friend. It certainly is nice to see you again. How was your trip? Did you have a good time?"

"The trip was good," I said. "It can be a little rough living in a motel room, but I made it safe and sound. Sir, I thought you were just passing through. I'm surprised to see you here this morning."

"Oh, you never know about me," he chuckled. "I could turn up just about anywhere and at any time."

We talked for half an hour about my job and various other subjects. Eventually he said, "Since we've crossed paths again, would you like to take up where we left off? I've found more proofs that God exists. The last time we talked, you still weren't convinced that God actually exists."

Not being one to mince words I answered, "No, sir, I don't."

There was a bit of surprise in his face. After a moment of silence, he asked, "Have I offended you, friend?"

"No, sir, you haven't. I'm sorry that I sounded so blunt. Please forgive me, sir, and let me explain."

With a look of relief, he said, "Whew. Thank goodness. You had me worried for a minute. Please continue, friend."

"Sir, if you remember, I made notes on all of your proofs. I took those notes with me on my trip with the intention of reading them a little closer. They made a certain amount of sense, but they just didn't go far enough to convince me that there is, in fact, a God. I was able to find objections to just about all of your proofs."

"Friend, they are not my proofs. If you remember, I told you that the proofs were from some great religious thinkers."

"Again, I am sorry, sir. I didn't mean to imply that they were your own proofs. Sometimes I am just a little too blunt. However, my point is that the proofs are not one hundred percent water tight."

"Friend, I thought you might say that. I was expecting such a response from you. Even though it is possible to voice legitimate objections to each and every proof, you might consider that when taken as a group, the proofs can weigh mightily toward ultimately proving the existence of God."

"Your point is well taken, sir, but when you add it all up, everything you've told me is merely an accumulation of theories developed by men."

"I'll give you that, my friend. They are theories indeed. But theories can be very convincing. A theory is based on certain assumptions that cannot be one hundred percent proven or validated. But in spite of that, we benefit from theories every day. We have real, material things in our lives as a result of the application of theories. Even though theories are not one hundred percent provable, they help us to have better lives. So, friend, is it really such a leap for you to believe these theories on God's existence?"

"Sir, you make a strong case for everything you say. But if you don't mind, I would like to be the teacher today. I am not as eloquent as you, but if you would bear with me, I believe I have something of importance to relate to you."

He looked at me with a little uncertainty in his face. Then after recovering he said, "Be my guest, friend. You certainly were attentive when *I* was the one doing the teaching. I'm anxious to hear what you have to say."

I swallowed hard and began, "Sir, I studied and considered all of your proofs. After a few days though, I gave up on finding an absolute proof of God's existence. Then one day I noticed a Bible in my room. I realized that you had exclusively promoted the thoughts and ideas of intelligent men, but not once had you referenced anything from the Bible, which is considered by many to be the Word of God. I decided to read the Bible and see if anything might stand out on its pages and convince me of the existence of God."

He hesitated for a few seconds. Then with a weak voice he said, "Okay, friend, what was your conclusion?"

"I read the Bible from cover to cover, making notes as I went. One night, I woke up with a sudden realization...no I woke up with a sudden *revelation* of God's existence."

He sat up straight in his chair and said, "This I've got to hear. Please, friend, tell me what you discovered."

I continued, "I'm warning you, sir, it's not going to be the kind of proofs you may be expecting to hear from me. I doubt that you would even call them proofs at all. There were several passages of scripture that stuck with me. I'll share a couple of them with you. There was one in which the disciple named Thomas said he would not believe that Jesus was raised from the dead unless he first saw Jesus with his own eyes. Eventually when Jesus appeared to him Thomas finally did believe, and he called Jesus his Lord and God. However, it doesn't appear to me that that Jesus was pleased with Thomas' doubt. Jesus more or less chided Thomas for requiring an absolute proof before he would believe. Jesus said that the ones who believe in Him without having to see Him are the ones who are truly blessed.[14] This chastisement made me think of my own situation. I had wanted undeniable proof before I would believe that there is a

God. But Jesus just wants me to simply believe in Him, and He wants me to simply accept Him in my heart."

"Are you sure about that?" asked the stranger. "I have been giving you strong proofs, which you have not accepted. Then while you were gone, you decided to accept a concept that is nowhere near a proof?"

"Yes, sir, I am sure. Another scripture speaks about a time when Jesus' disciples attempted to keep little children from pestering Him. Jesus rebuked the disciples and said that whoever doesn't receive the Kingdom of God as a little child, the same shall not be permitted to enter into His Kingdom.[15] This passage caused me to recall that a child doesn't normally question his father's authority. The child trusts his father and he blindly accepts what his father says as truth. God's Word tells us that He exists. We are expected to accept God's existence by faith, not by proof. We are not a judge and jury who must be presented a proof of his existence. He tells us that He exists. That's all we need to know. We are to trust what He tells us just as a child trusts his father."

The stranger just sat there, staring at me. I didn't know if he was mad or embarrassed or just speechless.

I was on a roll, so I continued by saying, "Over and over again, the Bible instructs us on one primary theme—that we are to simply believe in Him. We don't need proof; we don't need intelligent men to show Him to us; we don't need to see him face to face. Sir, we are to believe in Him and accept Him into our lives. Sir, while I was away, my life changed. I came to be a believer in God. I didn't become a believer because of your proofs. Instead, I became a believer because I simply made up my mind to become a believer. Sir, I have accepted Christ into my life. I am a new person."

Still, he sat in silence. I couldn't read his face. For all I knew, he might have been getting ready to reach across the table and hit me.

I went on, "Sir, please understand that I am not trying to ridicule you. I think your heart may be in the right place, but I believe that you are putting too much emphasis on the knowledge and intelligence of men. Sir, I suspect that you are not much different than I was. It looks to me like you decided to believe that God exists, only because of proofs that men have developed. I suspect that you believe, only so long as you have been provided a definitive proof of God's existence. I am reminded of passages in the Bible that tell us that the wisdom of this world is as foolishness with God.[16] Not once did you speak to me of anything that is written in God's Word. You only spoke from the vantage point of man's wisdom. As intelligent as some men are, they cannot begin to comprehend the nature of God. Now, sir, there is nothing wrong with using man's wisdom and knowledge—nothing whatsoever. Man's wisdom and knowledge is good, up to the limits placed on him by God. But in the end, regardless of man's knowledge, a person must make the decision to simply believe in God and accept Him by faith."

The stranger may as well have been a statue. He sat rigidly in his chair. His eyes didn't move. His face didn't change. He never even touched his coffee.

Swallowing hard, I continued, "I can't really put my finger on it, sir. But that's the beauty of accepting Christ. He wants us to accept him by faith, not by fact. If he expected us to accept him only after absolute facts were presented to us, he would have made us like mindless little toy soldiers. He would have programmed us to believe that he is the master and maker of all that is and that we are to believe in him and accept him because he told us to, and we have no other choice in the matter."

Silence was the only thing coming from the other side of the table.

I was in too deep to back out so I continued, "You, sir, have based your own belief that God exists on man's wisdom and knowledge. I am not suggesting that the theories you presented to me are wrong. I am not suggesting that those great thinkers are wrong. As a matter of fact, I believe those men were great men of God. I am not suggesting that man's knowledge and wisdom shouldn't be taught. What I am suggesting is that belief in God should have its roots in the Word of God. Then and only then, man's wisdom can be presented as a supplement to God's Word. Then, after you have accepted Him, you should turn around and tell others about Him, using God's Word as the basis, and man's wisdom as a supplement."

Breaking his silence, he said, "You've certainly developed quite an opinion."

"Yes, sir, I have. I have determined that the central theme of God's Word is that you are to make the decision within your heart to believe in God. After you accept Jesus into your heart by faith, you will receive salvation. He made you with a free will. He wants you to use your own free will to choose to believe in him. He wants you to accept him unconditionally. He doesn't want you to attempt to prove that He exists by way of man's wisdom and intelligence. No, sir, he wants you to accept him by faith."[17]

Appearing to be somewhat humbled he said, "Do you have any more to say, my friend?"

"Yes, sir, I do. Sir, you believe there *is* a God. I believe *in* God."

"Well, friend, it sounds like we both believe the same thing."

"Respectfully, sir, I don't believe we do. Even the devils believe there is a God.[18] Sir, you only believe with your mind that God exists. On the other hand, I believe *in* God. I believe with my heart. Sir, please don't take offense at this, but I suspect that your belief is rejected by God, while my belief is accepted by God."

"Friend, now you're going out a limb. Do you have an explanation for that last statement?"

"I'll try, sir. When a person merely believes something, they only passively believe. But, when a person believes *in* something, they actively believe."

"Is there a difference, my friend?"

"Sir, when people believe *in* something, they become actively involved *in* their belief. They join forces with others of like belief. They promote their belief. They sell their belief. They defend their belief. They are activists. Suppose that we have an elected leader who is suspected of being involved in corruption. Anyone can believe that the corrupt leader should be removed from office. But activists take their belief to the next level. They organize, they march, they take their belief to the streets, and they make their voices heard. Things may get so far out of hand that the government is forced to bring in law enforcement personnel to maintain peace and civility. Due to belief with action behind it, the leader is likely to be removed from office. Passive believers don't get anything done. Active believers advance their cause. Sir, you passively believe, but you're not actually promoting the Kingdom of God. All you have done is tell me that God exists from an academic point of view. Back in Jesus' day, most of the Pharisees, priests, and other Jewish religious rulers did not accept Jesus Christ. However, there were certain ones among them who actually did believe that He was the Son of God. However, they so enjoyed being praised by the people, that they would not openly admit that they believed in Christ.[19] Sir, I believe they were passive believers, just as you are. Jesus tells us that there is no way to get into the Kingdom of God except through Him.[20] Sir, God is love, first and foremost. We cannot see love and we cannot touch love. We can only feel love. God's love is all around us and in us. We don't need to see God to know He exists. We only need to experience his love for us. Then we will know He exists."

"Friend, you are definitely frank and to the point."

"Believe me, sir, I am telling you this with utmost humility. I would like to suggest that you do what I did. I realized that Jesus became the Sacrificial Lamb of God who takes away the sins of the world.[21] You, sir, need to believe in Him and accept Him into your own heart. When you do, you, too, will be a changed person.[22] God will live within you. He will be a part of your very being."[23]

"You have certainly stated your case with conviction. Friend, I am impressed. You've become a different person since I last saw you."

"Yes, sir, I have. Sir, may I ask one last thing?"

"I'm afraid to say yes after the beating I just received from you, but go ahead."

"Sir, I have two requests to make. First, I would like to formally ask you to accept Jesus into your heart and become one of his followers. Secondly, I would like for you and I to become friends. Do you realize that we have never been formally introduced to each other? My name is Bill. May I ask yours?"

His face began glowing. I thought I had embarrassed him. Was it because I told him his teachings were wrong, or was it because he had never asked my name? But then, I realized that his face was not turning red. Instead, his face was turning white. I wondered if he was about to faint. No, he couldn't be about to faint. If he were, he would be taking on a somewhat ashen appearance. Instead, he seemed to be glistening in the brightest and whitest hue I had ever seen. Whiter and brighter he became, so bright I had to start shielding my eyes. Not just his face, but his whole body, clothing and all were glowing. The whole room was bright. I could never have imagined a brighter or a whiter white. I was in such a shock I couldn't find any words to say. I may as well have had cotton in my mouth. Then I began to notice scars about his forehead, and horrible gashes in his hands.

Eventually it came to me that sitting right in front of me was none other than Jesus Christ himself. After an eternity of moments, I managed to find the strength to speak, "Jesus, is that you?"

"It is I, my friend. I am the God of Abraham, Isaac, and Jacob."[24]

After another long and painful silence, I asked, "Lord, was it you who met with me all of those mornings right here in this coffee shop?"

"Yes, my friend. It was I."

"And Lord, was it you who explained to me all of those proofs of God's existence?"

"Yes, my friend. It was me."

"I feel terrible, Lord. I just got through correcting you, and yet you sat there and listened to me. Lord, why didn't you reveal yourself to me on the very first day? Why did we have to go through all of those conversations? Lord, I was never convinced by those proofs. I finally became convinced when I searched for you in the Word of God. What if I had never picked up a Bible and searched for more?"

"Friend, I only answer that which has been asked. On the very first day, you said that no person had ever given you an absolute proof of God's existence. You said that you would believe only if someone could furnish you with undeniable facts."

"Yes, Lord. So why didn't you show yourself to me?"

"I answered the questions you asked. You wanted man's ideas. I gave you man's ideas. You were not really seeking me. You were merely looking for a scientific proof that I existed. Had you told me that you were seeking God and wanted to know God, I would have answered you differently. You now know me because you blindly accepted me, just as would a child."

I was astonished at my foolishness. The Maker of all things had been sitting at my table day after day after day. But I was not able to *know* him as long I attempted to understand him using the knowledge and wisdom of mankind. It was only after I accepted him by faith that I actually came to know him.

As quickly as he had begun glowing, he started fading from my sight. With fear gripping me, I said, "Lord, where are you going? Are you leaving me, just at the very moment I found you?"

Still fading, he replied, "Friend, you didn't find me today."

Confused and trembling I said, "Lord, it was just a few minutes ago that you appeared to me."

"Friend, I appeared to you a few minutes ago, but you found me back in that motel room. Now, I must go. There are others who are seeking me."

"But, Lord, please don't leave me now. I have so many questions. What about rules and regulations? How am I to know what I should and should not do? How do I know how to live my life?"

I was struggling to see him. I could just barely make out his image as he answered, "Now that you have accepted me in your life, I live within you. I am a part of your very being. So long as you love me and love your neighbor, you will have me with you as your guide. When you truly live for me, when you have me living within you, you will have no trouble knowing how to obey my laws. You will know within your heart if a thing is right or wrong; you will know instinctively what you must do. Tell me, friend, do you have to hold on to anything in order to keep yourself from floating out of your chair and up into the sky?"

"No, Lord, I stay on the ground because of the law of gravity."

"That's right, my friend. You are obeying the law of gravity right now, not because you are obeying written rules, but because you are an integral part of this earth's system and its physical laws. If you were to ride in a rocket ship out into the vast reaches of space, you would no longer be bound by earth's gravitational laws. You would be free of the law of gravity and you would float about in space. Likewise, as long as you are truly in the Kingdom of God, you will obey my laws. Do you remember the story of Peter walking on the water?"

"Yes, Lord."

"As long as Peter kept his eyes on me, he had the power to walk on water just as I did. It was only when he took his eyes off of me and focused his eyes on all that was around him that he began to sink into the sea.[25] Just as Peter had the power to walk on water, you have the power to obey my laws. All you have to do is keep your eyes and your heart focused on me. It is only when you take your eyes off of me that you will begin to disobey my laws. Keep your eyes and your devotion on me and you won't have to wonder about whether or not you are doing the right thing."

"But, Lord, I want you to be close to me."

"Even though you won't see me, I will be closer than a brother to you."[26]

Then he was gone. His chair was empty. The room lost its brightness. It must have been fifteen minutes before I managed to struggle out of my chair. I stumbled up to the store manager and asked, "What did you think about that?"

He answered, "What did I think about what?"

"The brightness in the room, the man at my table who just disappeared."

"I saw nothing unusual. No one disappeared. What exactly are you talking about?"

"Are you telling me you saw nothing unusual just now?'

"No, sir, I did not. I've been here all morning and nothing out of the ordinary has happened."

"What about the man I have been talking to for days on end? What did you think about him?"

"Sir, you have been a good customer. However, lately you *have* been acting a bit strange. You always come in alone and you leave alone, but lately you have acted as if you were with someone. The funny thing about it is that you have been gesturing and talking as if someone was at your table with you.

It's been rather amusing actually. The other customers didn't seem to mind because you never got loud or out of line."

I stood there for a moment with my mouth open. I could not believe what I just heard from the store manager. "You never saw me with another person?" I asked.

"Not one time," answered the store manager. "You are the ultimate loner."

■ ■ ■

I left the store and went on to work. For about a week, I went back to the coffee shop hoping to see Him again. Much to my disappointment, I never saw Him again.

For days on end, I replayed all of our encounters and conversations. I attempted to gain a better understanding of our conversations in the light of knowing that instead of speaking to a stranger all of those days, I was actually speaking to my Lord. I thought back to the many times I referred to him as a stranger, and I remembered that He always called me His friend. It was then that I realized that until I came to know him personally, He actually was a stranger to me. But through all of those days of conversation, He always called me his friend. *Why was that,* I wondered. Then I was reminded of the scriptures that tell us that the righteous ones are called the friend of God.[27] Perhaps He had the foreknowledge that I was about to believe on Him and accept Him in my heart.

The Mission

Because that which may be known of God is
manifest in them; for God hath shewed it unto
them. For the invisible things of him from the
creation of the world are clearly seen, being
understood by the things that are made, even his
eternal power and Godhead; so that they are
without excuse.

Romans 1:19-20 (KJV)

God is more truly imagined than expressed, and
He exists more truly than He is imagined.

Saint Augustine[28]

A few weeks later I received notice that I was to be
permanently transferred to the new office on the East Coast. The
daily ritual of visiting my favorite coffee shop came to an end.

∎ ∎ ∎

Occasionally I have an opportunity to return to my hometown on business. Before heading back East, I usually visit my old coffee shop one more time. I no longer expect to see Him at my table, but I enjoy sitting down and remembering the conversations I once had with the stranger, who became my Savior.

It's not often that I tell people about the day I met my Lord face to face. I have learned that people tend to excuse themselves from my presence rather quickly when I say such things.

∎ ∎ ∎

Now days, I am less driven by ritual. I visit various coffee shops. I make myself friendly with others. I now have a smile on my face, not unlike that of the stranger. Now, it is me who begins conversations with other people. I have learned from my own mistakes. Through conversations, I lead others to ask themselves if they know Jesus and if they have a personal relationship with Him. I encourage them to direct their thoughts and desires toward accepting Jesus into their lives. This has been a wonderful journey.

I keep my spiritual eyes focused on Jesus. As long as He is my passion, I can rest assured that I am actively involved in the

Kingdom of God. I tell people about the Gospel of Jesus Christ. I tell them that He loved them before the foundation of the world and that He is the sacrificial lamb that saves the world from its sins.

Sometimes I think back to the Wager spoken of by the stranger and how every person will either choose to believe he exists or choose not to believe he exists. There is a great irony to that Wager. During life, every person can make a personal choice to believe or not to believe. But a day will come when, at the judgment, every person who made a decision not to believe, will confess with their mouths that He does in fact exist.[29]

I am on a mission. My mission is to introduce everyone I meet to the Lord Jesus Christ. I ask them to choose to believe in Him and accept Him into their lives. Then they, too, will be assured of an eternal life with Jesus.

I have a mission. You have a mission. We are to love the Lord our God with all our hearts, and we are to love our neighbor as ourselves.[30] When we do, we will be obeying His call to be fishers of men. We will be helping those in need. We will be feeding the hungry. We will be ministering to the distressed. We will be visiting the sick. We will be visiting those in prison. We will be encouraging the down hearted. We will be sharing the Gospel.[31]

I have learned that religion is not accomplished by the act of sitting in a church. We go to church for fellowship, teaching, and encouragement, but that is not our purpose. Pure religion is caring for others.[32]

Will others physically see Jesus as I did? I can't say for sure that *I* physically saw Jesus that day. Perhaps it was a dream. Perhaps it was a vision. It doesn't matter whether or not I actually saw Jesus with my own eyes. What does matter is that I saw Him with my heart. I am walking with Jesus by faith, not by sight.[33] No, the people we witness to may not physically see Jesus, but I can tell you with certainty that they will see Jesus through us. When we truly love our neighbor; when we feed, clothe, visit and care for our neighbor, we are doing those things directly for, and directly to our Lord. When we love our neighbor and share His Good News, they will see Jesus in us. When they look on us, they will be looking on Jesus.

There once was a time when I had a series of Conversations with a Stranger.

That Stranger became my Savior

Now, I'm on a mission

Would you join me on that mission?

Epilogue

Every Christian has at least one ministry. Whether we have one ministry or many, we all have one ministry in common. First and foremost, our ministry is where we are in our station of life. The business owner has the capacity to help his fellow man by providing goods, services, training, or support to those in need. The employee, the retiree, the student, and the stay-at-home person have the ability to provide encouragement, personal support, and mentoring to those they come in contact with. *All* Christians are expected to share the Gospel. No one is expected to limit their walk with God through worship alone. We are expected to both worship *and* serve our God. We serve God through our interactions with others.

Notes to the Text

The Wager

[1] Pascal's Wager

Blaise Pascal was a French mathematician, physicist, and religious philosopher in the 1600s. He developed the probability theory, which applies to and influences gambling and economics.

Pascal's Wager suggests that it is better to gamble on believing in God than not to believe in God.

According to Pascal, God either exists or he doesn't. There are no other options. Therefore, mathematically speaking there is at least a 50% probability that God exists. Consequently, since belief in a God that actually exists will result in eternal life, the wisest choice for mankind is to live out one's life as if God does exist. If right, a person will gain eternal life. If wrong, nothing is lost. So, only a fool would choose to live a Godless life.

A.   As for the existence of God, there are only two possibilities:

    1.   God exists

2. God does not exist

B.   As for belief in God, there also are only two choices:

1. You believe in God

2. You don't believe in God

The wager you make is your belief or non-belief in God and how you live your life as a consequence of your believing or not believing in God.

The winnings or outcome of the wager is what occurs or does not occur after death. The person talking to the stranger in this book does not know whether God exists or not. Consequently, he does not yet buy into the concept of heaven or hell. But, for considering this wager, he applies the common belief held by Christians regarding heaven and hell.

The wager possibilities are as follows:

1. You will live as if God does exist

2. You will live as if God does not exist

There are four possible variations in the wager:

1. If you live as if God exists, and in fact He does exist, then your outcome will be eternal life with God in heaven.

Your outcome is positive.

2. If you live as if God exists, and in fact He does not exist, then your outcome will be nothing (when you die, you merely cease to exist).

Your outcome is neutral—no loss, no gain.

3. If you live as if God does not exist, and in fact He does exist, then your outcome will be an eternal existence in hell.

Your outcome is negative.

4. If you live as if God does not exist, and in fact He does not exist, then your outcome will be nothing (when you die, you merely cease to exist).

Your outcome is neutral—no loss, no gain.

Mathematically, there is a 50% chance that God does exist. When coupled with the philosophical proofs described in this book, there is a much greater than 50% chance that God exists. (This is based simply on human intelligence and mathematics. It does not take into account the simple faith we should actually utilize in our belief in God.)

Of all four outcomes, two are neutral, one is negative, and one is positive. Considering that there is only one positive outcome, and considering that there is a greater than 50% chance that God does exist, only a fool would refuse to live his life as if God does, in fact, exist.

The Mover

[2] Argument from Motion

The Argument from Motion is St. Thomas Aquinas' First Way. St. Thomas Aquinas was a Christian philosopher in the 1200s. His Argument from Motion is based on the observation that any object in motion had to have had some other object or force to put it into motion.

An interpretation of his argument is as follows:

1. Whatever is in motion is put in motion by something else.

2. Whatever put that object in motion must itself be put in motion by something else.

3. Through a chain of events, each object moving another object must have been moved by yet another object farther in the past.

4. There cannot be an endless chain of moving events going on to infinity.

5. Without a first mover, there would be no motion.

6. Therefore, it is necessary to arrive at a first mover: a first mover put in motion by no other.

7. This first mover is God.

The Beginning

[3] Was there a specific beginning?

> In the beginning God created the heaven and the earth.
> And the earth was without form, and void; and darkness was upon the face of the deep.

> Genesis 1:1 (KJV)

God always was and God always has been. God is without time. The above scripture is referring to the beginning of creation as we know it.

Mankind often attempts to explain the beginning of time and the beginning of our universe. One of those thoughts is that our universe is infinitely old; it had no specific beginning. Another thought is that it had its beginning in the "big bang."

As explained in this chapter, any determination that our universe is infinitely old is a false conclusion.

The scientific world is beginning to put forth the theory that the universe began as the "big bang." Can the "big bang" theory coincide with the Christian concept of Creation? First of all, science is the understanding and application of the laws of nature. Sometimes science does not have a firm grip on those laws, so they are called theories. One such theory is the "big bang." God is all powerful and able to do all things. He could create all things gradually as the "big bang" suggests, just as easily as He could create all things all at once. Who really knows if the earth, the moon, the sun, and all other heavenly bodies fully existed all at once on the day of creation or if God caused billions and billions of particles to begin accumulating together over time until they became the universe as we know it?

However, it was that God created the universe, we can stand on one fact: our universe did have a specific beginning.

The Cause

[4] The Argument from Cause

The Causation of Existence is St. Thomas Aquinas' Second Way. A similar philosophy is also discussed by St. Augustine. They argue that no object is capable of creating its own self. Every created object had to be created by something or someone else. Going back in time, there had to be the first creator. This first creator *could not itself, have been created.* St. Thomas Aquinas uses the term "cause" or "caused." This term is interchangeable with "creator" or "created."

An interpretation of his argument goes as follows:

1. All things and beings that exist are caused by other things.

2. No thing can be the cause of its own self. If so, it would exist prior to itself.

3. Through a chain of events, each object or being causing the existence of another object or being must have been caused by yet another object or being.

4. There cannot be an endless chain of objects or beings causing the existence of other objects of beings.

5. Without a first cause, there would be no objects or beings in existence today.

6. Therefore, it is necessary to arrive at a first cause: a first cause that is caused by no other.

7. This first cause is God.

The Necessary

[5] Henri Frederic Ameil. A Critic in the 1800s.

[6] The Argument from Contingent and Necessary Objects

The argument of Contingent and Necessary Objects is St. Thomas Aquinas' Third Way. There are only two kinds of objects in existence: contingent beings and necessary beings. A contingent being is an object or being that cannot exist without a necessary being causing its existence. The necessary being is God.

An interpretation of his argument goes as follows:

1. We find things (beings) are possible to be and possible not to be.

2. That which is possible not to be, at some time is not.

3. If everything is possible not to be, then at one time there could have been nothing in existence.

4. If there was a time when nothing was in existence, then even now there would be nothing in existence because that which does not exist only begins to exist by something else already existing.

5. Therefore, not all beings are merely possible.

6. There must exist something, the existence of which is necessary.

7. This necessary being must have of itself its own necessity, not receiving it from another.

8. This necessary being is God.

The Perfect

[7] Robert Browning. An English poet in the 1800s.

[8] The Perfect One

The Perfect One is St. Thomas Aquinas' Fourth Way.   The qualities of all things are judged by something else.

An interpretation of his argument goes as follows:

1. Everything that exists has certain qualities, such as: whiteness, greatness, and goodness.

2. Among beings, there are some that are more or less of certain qualities, such as: more or less good, true, great, tall, large, and hot.

3. For something to be more or less of a certain quality, there must exist something that is the ultimate of that quality, such as: the hottest, the largest, the best, the tallest, and the whitest.

4. If anything is great, there must exist something that is the greatest. If anything is hot, there must exist something that is the hottest. If anything is good, there must exist something that is the most good.

5. Among things in existence, any thing that seems to contain the greatest of a certain quality will eventually be replaced by another thing that contains an even greater of that certain quality.

6. There must exist something that expresses the greatest of all qualities by which all other things are judged and compared.

7. This being that expresses the greatest of all qualities is the Perfect One.

8. The Perfect One is God.

The Intelligent Designer

[9] The Intelligent Designer is St. Thomas Aquinas' Fifth Way. A similar philosophy is found in Paley's Teleological Argument. This argument suggests that all things must be designed by an intelligent designer.

An interpretation of his argument goes as follows:

1. There are things which lack intelligence.

2. Nevertheless, these things act for an end, by acting in the same way, so as to obtain the best result.

3. It is by design that they act in such a manner as to achieve their end.

4. Whatever lacks intelligence cannot move toward an end on its own. It must be directed by some being endowed with knowledge and intelligence.

5. Therefore, some intelligent being exists by whom all things are directed to their end.

6. This Intelligent Being is God.

The Greater

[10] Richard Garnett. An English author in the 1800s.

[11] The Greater is St. Anselm's Ontological Argument. St. Anselm was a Christian philosopher around the year 1100 AD. His argument is based on reason alone.

His argument goes as follows:

1. God is a being in which none greater is possible.

2. The concept of God exists in one's mind.

3. It is possible that God may also exist in reality.

4. It is greater for a thing to exist in both the mind and in reality, than in the mind alone.

5. If God exists in the mind only, then a greater than God could be thought, because one could think of God in reality, in addition to being in the mind alone.

6. It cannot be that God exists in the mind only, because God is a being in which a greater is not possible.

7. Therefore, God exists in the mind and in reality.

The Parting

[12] John Gay. An English playwright and poet.

The Revelation

[13] St. Anselm was a British philosopher around the turn of the second century AD.

The Light

[14] Thomas believed only after presented with absolute proof.

Then the same day at evening, being the first *day* of the week, when the doors were shut where the disciples were assembled for fear of the Jews, came Jesus and stood in the midst, and saith unto them, Peace *be* unto you. And when he had so said, he shewed unto them *his* hands and his side. Then were the disciples glad, when they saw the Lord. Then said Jesus to them again, Peace *be* unto you: as *my* Father hath sent me, even so send I you. And when he had said this, he breathed on *them*, and saith unto them, Receive ye the Holy Ghost: Whose soever sins ye remit, they are remitted unto them; *and* whose soever *sins* ye retain, they are retained. But Thomas, one of the twelve, called Didymus, was not with them when Jesus came. The other disciples therefore said unto him, We have seen the Lord. But he said unto them, Except I shall see in his hands the print of the nails, and put my finger into the print of the nails, and thrust my hand into his side, I will not believe. And after eight days again his disciples were within, and Thomas with them: *then* came Jesus, the doors being shut, and stood in the midst, and said, Peace *be* unto you. Then saith he to Thomas, Reach hither thy finger, and behold my hands; and reach hither thy hand, and thrust *it* into my side: and be not faithless, but believing. And Thomas answered and said unto him, My Lord and my God. Jesus saith unto him, Thomas, because thou hast seen me, thou hast believed: blessed *are* they that have not seen, and *yet* have believed.

John 20:19-29 (KJV)

[15] Instruction to receive the Kingdom of God just as would a child.

And they brought young children to him, that he should touch them: and *his* disciples rebuked those that brought *them*. But when Jesus saw *it*, he was much displeased, and said unto them, Suffer the little children to come unto me, and forbid them not: for of such is the kingdom of God. Verily I say unto you, Whosoever shall not receive the kingdom of God as a little child, he shall not enter therein. And he took them up in his arms, put *his* hands upon them, and blessed them.

Mark 10:13-16 (KJV)

[16] God's wisdom versus man's wisdom.

Because the foolishness of God is wiser than men; and the weakness of God is stronger than men.

1 Corinthians 1:25 (KJV)

For the wisdom of this world is foolishness with God. For it is written, He taketh the wise in their own craftiness.

1 Corinthians 3:19 (KJV)

It is better to trust in the LORD than to put confidence in man.

Psalms 118:8 (KJV)

Trust in the LORD with all thine heart; and lean not unto thine own understanding.

Proverbs 3:5 (KJV)

[17] Faith in God is necessary.

(For we walk by faith, not by sight:)

2 Corinthians 5:7 (KJV)

But without faith *it is* impossible to please *him*: for he that cometh to God must believe that he is, and *that* he is a rewarder of them that diligently seek him.

Hebrews 11:6 (KJV)

That if thou shalt confess with thy mouth the Lord Jesus, and shalt believe in thine heart that God hath raised him from the dead, thou shalt be saved.

Romans 10:9 (KJV)

For by grace are ye saved through faith; and that not of yourselves: *it is* the gift of God:

Ephesians 2:8 (KJV)

That whosoever believeth in him should not perish, but have eternal life.

John 3:15 (KJV)

Verily, verily, I say unto you, He that heareth my word, and believeth on him that sent me, hath everlasting life, and shall not come into condemnation; but is passed from death unto life.

John 5:24 (KJV)

[18] Believing that there *is* a God is not enough.

Thou believest that there is one God; thou doest well: the devils also believe, and tremble.

James 2:19 (KJV)

[19] Some of the chief rulers believed on Christ.

Nevertheless among the chief rulers also many believed on him; but because of the Pharisees they did not confess *him*, lest they should be put out of the synagogue: For they loved the praise of men more than the praise of God.

John 12:42-43 (KJV)

[20] Jesus is the Door

Verily, verily, I say unto you, He that entereth not by the door into the sheepfold, but climbeth up some other way, the same is a thief and a robber. But he that entereth in by the door is the shepherd of the sheep. To him the porter openeth; and the sheep hear his voice: and he calleth his own sheep by name, and leadeth them out. And when he putteth forth his own sheep, he goeth before them, and the sheep follow him: for they know his voice. And a stranger will they not follow, but will flee from him: for they know not the voice of strangers. This parable spake Jesus unto them: but they understood not what things they were which he spake unto them. Then said Jesus unto them again, Verily, verily, I say unto you, I am the door of the sheep. All that ever came before me are thieves and robbers: but the sheep did not hear them. I am the door: by me if any man enter in, he shall be saved, and shall go in and out, and find pasture.

John 10:1-9 (KJV)

[21] Jesus is the Sacrificial Lamb.

The next day John seeth Jesus coming unto him, and saith, Behold the Lamb of God, which taketh away the sin of the world.

John 1:29 (KJV)

[22] Accepting and confessing Christ is the key to salvation.

That if thou shalt confess with thy mouth the Lord Jesus, and shalt believe in thine heart that God hath raised him from the dead, thou shalt be saved.

Romans 10:9 (KJV)

[23] He lives within us.

At that day ye shall know that I *am* in my Father, and ye in me, and I in you.

John 14:20 (KJV)

[24] Jesus is the God of our fathers.

And Thomas answered and said unto him, My Lord and my God.

John 20:28 (KJV)

But as touching the resurrection of the dead, have ye not read that which was spoken unto you by God saying, I am the God of Abraham, and the God of Isaac, and the God of Jacob? God is not the God of the dead, but of the living.

Matthew 22:31-32 (KJV)

[25] Peter walking on water

And in the fourth watch of the night Jesus went unto them, walking on the sea. And when the disciples saw him walking on the sea, they were troubled, saying, It is a spirit; and they cried out for fear. But straightway Jesus spake unto them, saying, Be of good cheer; it is I; be not afraid. And Peter answered him and said, Lord, if it be thou, bid me come unto thee on the water. And

---

he said, Come. And when Peter was come down out of the ship, he walked on the water, to go to Jesus. But when he saw the wind boisterous, he was afraid; and beginning to sink, he cried, saying, Lord, save me. And immediately Jesus stretched forth *his* hand, and caught him, and said unto him, O thou of little faith, wherefore didst thou doubt?

Matthew 14:25-31 (KJV)

[26] Jesus is a friend that is closer than a brother.

A man that hath friends must shew himself friendly: and there is a friend that sticketh closer than a brother.

Proverbs 18:24 (KJV)

[27] We are called His friend.

Henceforth I call you not servants; for the servant knoweth not what his lord doeth: but I have called you friends; for all things that I have heard of my Father I have made known unto you.

John 15:15 (KJV)

For what saith the scripture? Abraham believed God, and it was counted unto him for righteousness.

Romans 4:3 (KJV)

And he received the sign of circumcision, a seal of the righteousness of the faith which *he had yet* being uncircumcised: that he might be the father of all them that believe, though they be not circumcised; that righteousness might be imputed unto them also: And the father of circumcision to them who are not of the circumcision only, but who also walk in the steps of that faith of our father Abraham, which *he had* being *yet* uncircumcised. For the promise, that he should be the heir of the world, *was* not to Abraham, or to his seed, through the law, but through the righteousness of faith.

Romans 4:11-13 (KJV)

And the scripture was fulfilled which saith, Abraham believed God, and it was imputed unto him for righteousness: and he was called the Friend of God.

James 2:23 (KJV)

The Mission

[28] St. Augustine was a religious figure in the first century, AD.

[29] Even those who choose not to believe will one day confess Jesus.

For it is written, *As* I live, saith the Lord, every knee shall bow to me, and every tongue shall confess to God.

Romans 14:11 (KJV)

[30] Summation of God's Law

Jesus said unto him, Thou shalt love the Lord thy God with all thy heart, and with all thy soul, and with all thy mind. This is the first and great commandment. And the second *is* like unto it, Thou shalt love thy neighbour as thyself. On these two commandments hang all the law and the prophets.

Matthew 22:37-40 (KJV)

[31] Our love for God is shown by our love for our neighbor.

Then shall the King say unto them on his right hand, Come, ye blessed of my Father, inherit the kingdom prepared for you from the foundation of the world: For I was an hungred, and ye gave me meat: I was thirsty, and ye gave me drink: I was a stranger, and ye took me in: Naked, and ye clothed me: I was sick, and ye visited me: I was in prison, and ye came unto me. Then shall the righteous answer him, saying, Lord, when saw we thee an hungred, and fed *thee*? or thirsty, and gave *thee* drink? When saw we thee a stranger, and took *thee* in? or naked, and clothed *thee*?

Or when saw we thee sick, or in prison, and came unto thee? And the King shall answer and say unto them, Verily I say unto you, Inasmuch as ye have done *it* unto one of the least of these my brethren, ye have done *it* unto me.

Matthew 25:34-40 (KJV)

[32] Pure Religion

Pure religion and undefiled before God and the Father is this, To visit the fatherless and widows in their affliction, *and* to keep himself unspotted from the world.

James 1:27 (KJV)

[33] Faith in Him

Therefore we are always confident, knowing that, whilst we are at home in the body, we are absent from the Lord: (For we walk by faith, not by sight:).

2 Corinthians 5:6-7 (KJV)

Made in the USA
Coppell, TX
16 June 2021